THE ULTIMATE WEAPON IS PRAYER

"Inviting Heaven to Intervene in Earthly Affairs"

Sr. Pastor Teresa S. McCurry

Printed in the United States of America

First Printing, August 2021

ISBN: 978-1-7338770-6-0

MCCURRY MINISTRIES INTERNATIONAL

CONTENTS

FOREWORD

I *remember the day Teresa* McCurry showed up in my virtual office. In a world where darkness, gloom and bad news are so readily dispersed, she was a bright light. Her effervescent personality radiated with the goodness of God. The purity of her desire to know the Lord in a deeper way and to see others grow in knowledge and wisdom was a much-needed breath of fresh air. Her passion and hunger for the things of the Lord were tangible and could not be contained. Since that initial meeting, as I've grown to know Teresa, I've also grown to know this truth; Teresa McCurry is a woman of prayer.

Prayer is one of the most critical aspects of our Christian walks, it must be developed and maintained for prime growth in Christ.

The importance of the power of prayer and having a healthy prayer life can never be understated. Prayer is our direct pipeline to the

Father and is the conduit by which we get to know and understand His heart. It's how we invoke Heaven to move on earth.

While most believers know to pray, many are often lacking in how to pray. Teresa has grabbed hold of the revelation of both the knowing and the how, and in doing so has stepped into a level of authority that most don't reach. She has masterfully taken this revelation and communicated it in a simple, understandable yet profoundly power way through her book, The Ultimate Weapon Is Prayer.

This is more than just a book; **IT IS A CLARION CALL TO PRAYER**. It is a training manual to help cultivate and develop a deeper level of prayer and is a catalyst for greater anticipation of answer to prayer. It is a power tool and as the title implies, the Ultimate Weapon to inviting heaven to intervene in our earthly affairs. As you walk through each chapter, you will come away with a greater revelation of the importance and power of a committed prayer life and how to skillfully use this ultimate weapon.

This book will create paradigm shifts for believers at all stages of their Christian life. For those who are new to the faith, it provides for them dynamic keys that will aid them in their beginning walk with the Lord. For the maturing Christian, it will help them regain focus on their prayer life, and for all it will unlock the wisdom and authority that God designed prayer to provide us.

Thank you, Teresa, for saying yes to the call to prayer I highly recommend this book to believers everywhere.

Dr. Tony Robinson
Tony Robinson Consulting
THE PROPHETIC COLLECTIVE
DAUGHTERS OF THE WELL
tonyrcoaching.com

Introduction

Our need for prayer is a result of the way God arranged dominion and authority for the earth. God made the world, Then He made men and women and gave them dominion over all the works of His hands. Man was created to be the "god" of this world. He was given full authority in the earth realm, and God will not supersede that authority. This means that when God said, "Let them rule...over all the earth," He was ordering the dominion of the world in such a way as to make the rule of humans essential for the accomplishment of His purposes. He causes things to happen on earth when men and women are in agreement with His will. Prayer, therefore, is essential for God's will to be done in the earth.—Myles Monroe, *Understanding the Purpose and Power of Prayer*

I *used this quote at* the beginning of this book to help you understand nothing promised by God will come marching to your doorstep without praying for it.

We conquer in many ways by using our knees. Bow down as much as you can. Speak to God as much as you can. In this life, we must work to get a paycheck. If you have a son or daughter on a school's sports team, you will understand this even better. These children labor for weeks. Every day they are in the gym and on the playing field preparing to win the next game. To achieve what they want, they must put in the work.

Nothing in life is free. Everything has a cost. When athletes work out in the gym day in and day out, eventually, they meet their opponents, play the game and perhaps win. Their victory did not come about because they were lucky—not at all. It came by preparation. They put in the work and prepared much more than their opponents for the day. And as a result, they won.

It is the same with every human living on the earth who desires results from God through prayer. Praying is like the work you put in every day in the gym. It is like the weights you lift so you stay strong for the game day.

Thanks to Myles Munroe, I see prayer as an earthly license for heavenly interference. It is a license in the sense that without it, the dominion and earthly goodies God promised you in the Bible will not be realized. They will simply be words written thousands of years ago. However, for those who pray, these words are life and freedom.

This book is the second in a trilogy series. In the first book, I taught about the whole armor of God. It summarized what believers must put on to remain safe from the Devil's tactics against us.

It is a fitting reminder of the importance of wearing God's armor to win in life. I strongly encourage you to get a copy to know all of the Devil's tricks against believers. More importantly, to stand in the midst of attacks and let the Lord and His heavenly hosts fight on your behalf. The armor will work in your favor if you rightly apply each part to your everyday life.

Finally, my brethren, be strong in the Lord and in the power of His might. Put on the whole armor of God, that you may be able to stand against the wiles of the devil. For we do not wrestle against flesh and blood, but against principalities, against powers, against the rulers of the darkness of this age, against spiritual hosts of wickedness in the heavenly places. Therefore take up the whole armor of God, that you may be able to withstand in the evil day, and having done all, to stand. Stand therefore, having girded your waist with truth, having put on the breastplate of righteousness, and having shod your feet with the preparation of the gospel of peace; above all, taking the shield of faith with which you will be able to quench all the fiery darts of the wicked one. And take the helmet of salvation, and the sword of the Spirit, which is the word of God; praying always with all prayer and supplication in the Spirit, being watchful to this end with all perseverance and supplication for all the saints. (Ephesians 6:10-18, NKJV)

This second book of the trilogy series is based on the last verse of the passage above, Ephesians 6:18: *"Praying always with all prayer and supplication in the Spirit, being watchful to this end with all perseverance and supplication for all the saints."*

The focus of this book is on the weapon of prayer because of its importance to the life of a believer. Prayer is speaking to God. A healthy relationship is one with constant communication. Therefore, when you communicate with God, you are keeping your relationship with Him in great shape, and that works very well in your favor.

We see the consequences of poor or no communication in our homes every day. When parents and children have difficulty talking to each other, it usually results in hatred and all sorts of other negative emotions. The relationships are unproductive. On the contrary, when they communicate frequently, good relationships develop and great things happen!

Prayer is the master key that unlocks the door for great things to happen in your life. So get ready to refresh what you already know and to implement what you will learn in this book. Amen!

Chapter 1

PRAYER

**Prayer, a Weapon That Works
Well When Used Always**

She (my mother) became a warrior far superior to any epic hero. She became a giant on her knees. With a sword in one hand she battled the enemies of death and disease, and with her other hand stretched toward heaven she kept beseeching God's help and His mercy.
—Bishop T.D. Jakes

Rather than set aside daily time for prayer, I pray constantly and spontaneously about everything I encounter on a daily basis. When someone shares something with me, I'll often simply say, 'let's pray about this right now. —Thomas Kinkade

As I said earlier, this book focuses on prayer, different types of prayers, and what prayer can do in our lives. However, I decided to make this first chapter a lesson on the importance of praying always because through prayer, God's will is manifested here on the earth.

Prayer is having a conversation with God and should be made without ceasing (1 Thessalonians 5:16-18). As we grow in our love for Jesus Christ, we will naturally desire to talk to Him.

"Rejoice always, pray without ceasing, 18 in everything give thanks; for this is the will of God in Christ Jesus for you" (1 Thessalonians 5:16-18, NKJV).

Talking to God all the time must not intimidate you. You should also not grow weary of praying. When you talk to God about your situations, and He answers your prayer, it is between you and Him. Nobody knows about that situation. So, don't be shy about sharing your whole heart with Him. It will only be between you and God, no one else.

Our God is faithful, and He is calling us to a lifestyle of prayer accompanied by total trust in Him. Pray every day. Share your fears, failures, shortcomings, attitudes, success stories, and so forth with Him. I suggested you share many things with God because, as you will learn later in the book, you can pray for several things under what are called different prayer "themes."

God is calling for us to pray always

- Daniel prayed 3 times a day, so can you.
- Jesus prayed all night long, so can you.
- Paul said we should pray without ceasing: this is your mandate.
- Prayer is important; prayer is not an event. Prayer is a lifestyle. Live it. Love it.
- God answers prayer. Don't be shy to let Him know what's in your heart, always,
- Gideon prayed and God gave him directions. He will give you the same.
- Hannah prayed and God blessed her with a child after she was barren. Consistent prayer works.

- Elijah prayed and it did not rain for three years and six months.
- Elijah also prayed asking God to prove who He is and rain fire down from heaven
- Hezekiah received a word from the prophet that if he did not get his house in order, he would die. He turned to the wall, prayed, and cried out to God. God added fifteen more years to his life.
- Peter was in jail; the church prayed and he was released. You too can be released from what's tormenting you.
- Paul and Silas prayed and sang praises unto God. Immediately, all the prison doors were opened, and everyone's bands were loosed.

As you have seen, amazing things can happen to those who believe in prayer, practice, and live it in faith. Remember to always pray in faith, for it is impossible to please God without it (Hebrews 11:6).

Oh, yes, I can give testimonies from our local ministry. God is still answering prayers. Below are some miraculous experiences, which show God answers when His people are praying in faith.

- **My Husband Apostle Greg & Pastor Tee (Me)**
  We prayed and New Beginning Ministries is changing lives and renewing minds. The people of God are no longer just Word-reading but have been transformed into a Word-doing kind of people.

- **Pastor Denise** prayed and got healed. She had the symptoms of a stroke and was bleeding on the brain. Her blood pressure was off the Richter Scale. Her healing left the doctors baffled, but God does all these great things through prayer.

- **Sis Annette** prayed and cancer was evicted from her body.

- **Deacon Bob** prayed and now he has a "cancer-free testimony."

- **Elder Barb** was in a fight for good health for over three years. But now, she has a clean bill of health. To God be the glory.

- **Bro. Mike** was "toe up from the floor up." In other words, he was extremely intoxicated.

We prayed for him and he was filled with the Holy Spirit. God is still working in his life.

- **Sis Lolita** prayed when she was in trouble. God changed the law just to set her free. Indeed, He will leave the ninety-nine to come see about the one.

You must pray all the time. It brings the results you need and produces testimonies like the ones in the preceding paragraphs. God has done so many things for us if we were to speak about them, we would obviously run out of paper. But we are confident prayer works and should be done at all times.

Praying – this is giving God worship or to worship God.

When we pray, we are communicating with God and at the same time worshiping Him. We are telling God our hearts' desires and at the same time worshiping Him.

When we worship God in the midst of our challenges, which He turned into changes, we have a track record to refer to. In other words, we can look back at the times in our past when God delivered us and find courage and strength to trust Him in our present situations. We understand if He was faithful in our yesterdays, He can definitely handle our todays and tomorrows.

"Never stop praying" (1 Thessalonians 5:17, NLT).

"Pray without ceasing" (1 Thessalonians 5:17, KJV).

We have grown to know the King James Version of the preceding verse. However, I like how the NLT puts it in very simple terms: "Never stop praying." Why should you? Stay in constant communication with your maker, your creator, God.

"And pray in the Spirit on all occasions with all kinds of prayers and requests. With this in mind, be alert and always keep on praying for all the Lord's people" (Ephesians 6:18, NIV).

Praying must not come to an end. We must pray during the day and in all kinds of ways. Later in the book, we will discuss various kinds of prayers and how they will help you in different circumstances. You are in a good position to know about these kinds of prayers if you feed on the Word of God, the Bible. As you read the Bible, you will learn how to pray in various situations. Situations give birth to a variety of prayers. As such, stand guided; know how to pray at all times and in all circumstances.

> "But seek first his kingdom and his righteousness, and all these things will be given to you as well" (Matthew 6:33, NIV).

We must speak the word of the Lord with our mouths. *"Let the redeemed of the Lord say so"* (Psalm 107:2). This is exactly what you need to do. Open your mouth and speak the Word of the Lord. You can't just think it in your mind. Your thoughts are just that—thoughts, which translate to nothing when it comes to actions and results. Remember, prayer is an action you choose to take, and it comes with real results from heaven.

After Jesus ascended to heaven, He left us the Holy Spirit who makes intercession on our behalf with groanings that cannot be uttered (Romans 8:26). Even though the Spirit prays to God on our behalf, it does not mean we can get away with complacency. The Holy Spirit does not produce power in your thoughts (for the ones who choose not to pray). Rather, He produces power by the Word of God spoken out of your mouth.

Why We Must Pray Always

Life is an ongoing process; it never stops. One day you are a toddler; the next, you are in high school, and before you know it, you are planning to get married. Life keeps moving. Now, the greatest thing about all those stages is you require different things and various outcomes at every stage.

These outcomes and inputs for life are the things we are already given by God. But you ought to pray to Him first to unlock them in the present moment. When you are a child, you worry about just going to see your friends and that they like you. When you are in college, you are concerned about passing exams. When you get married, you are concerned about different things altogether. However, you find all these things are summarized in the promises of God being manifested. I say this because they all have a similar underlying value, which is to dominate our situations or our environments. When you go to see friends and want to feel loved and good while there, it means you desire to dominate those surroundings. Dominating does not mean being loud and controlling everything and everyone. It means having things in an environment that brings comfort and joy.

Therefore, if God already promised us good things, why haven't they manifested? I believe it is because we are not communicating with God on a regular basis as the Bible recommends.

> Then God said, "Let Us make man in Our image, according to Our likeness; let them have dominion/ control. over the fish of the sea, over the birds of the air, and over the cattle, over [a]all the earth and over every creeping thing that creeps on the earth." (Genesis 1:26, NKJV)

No need to add much to this scripture. The Bible says it all. God does not renege on His promises. If you think of the dominion we were given there is no reason to live in panic. But I do see a reason to pray always knowing the promises were already given by God who is faithful to see them come to pass.

- God gave us authority/control. If we need or want His help, we must ask Him for it knowing He delivers.

- God knows what your situation is.
- God knows what you are going through.
- God knows what you are up against.

Nevertheless, all these things can only be given to you when you ask for them. Remember Matthew Chapter 7.

> Ask and it will be given to you; seek and you will find; knock and the door will be opened to you. For everyone who asks receives; the one who seeks finds; and to the one who knocks, the door will be opened. "Which of you, if your son asks for bread, will give him a stone? Or if he asks for a fish, will give him a snake? If you, then, though you are evil, know how to give good gifts to your children, how much more will your Father in heaven give good gifts to those who ask him." (Matthew 7:7-11, NIV).

Looking at the Scriptures, I do not have much to add, except whenever you knock on that door and pray, you will be asking God to unlock the dominion you have been looking for and that He promised. As such, even if God is willing and ready to give, the words coming out of your mouth in prayer are the key to unlocking all of it.

In the following chapter, I will take you through a quick lesson about what prayer is, after which, we will examine the types of prayers we can use.

Chapter 2

WHAT IS PRAYER?

N ow, *it's time to* move ahead with understanding more about prayer. I pray that this will be a fruitful walk in the Word. I deliberately used the word "walk" to describe this journey, so you will know it is not something to be rushed through. When learning about anything in life, it is the ones who take their time studying every twist and turn who are successful. And for those who rush things through, it's never an easy journey.

To make communication with God your lifestyle, you must learn every important step to walking your way up to becoming a prayer warrior.

Learn as much as you can and carefully travel this road because it lasts for a lifetime.

In other words, I am saying run-walk this journey; it will need this from you. It takes power, courage, endurance, and faith as the main ingredients.

Above all else, you should put all your focus on one point to draw all the above qualities necessary to run-walk this journey. You will need this to become a warrior in prayer. We must fix your eyes on Jesus.

"Fixing our eyes on Jesus, the author and finisher of faith, who for the joy set before Him endured the cross, despising the shame, and has sat down at the right hand of the throne of God" (Hebrews 12:2, New American Standard Bible).

Having said that, I see no reason to continue reminding you Jesus Christ is important in your journey to live a life of prayer. Always focus on Him and you will understand what prayer is and what it takes to live a life full of prayer.

Moving ahead, I will show you more examples that reveal what prayer is and how it should be when we present it to God.

> Is anyone among you suffering? Let him pray. Is anyone cheerful? Let him sing psalms. Is anyone among you sick? Let him call for the elders of the church, and let them pray over him, anointing him with oil in the name of the Lord. And the prayer of faith will save the sick, and the Lord will raise him up. And if he has committed sins, he will be forgiven. Confess your trespasses to one another, and pray for one another, that you may be healed. The effective, [k]fervent prayer of a righteous man avails much. Elijah was a man with a nature like ours, and he prayed earnestly that it would not rain; and it did not rain on the land for three years and six months. And he prayed again, and the heaven gave rain, and the earth produced its fruit. (James 5:13-18, NKJV

This scripture verse reveals that what Jesus taught the disciples about prayer can be done by us.

James 5:13 starts with three questions:

1. Is anyone among you suffering?
   Here, suffering means experiencing a

difficult time. You are hurting physically, emotionally, mentally, financially, in your relationships or other circumstances.

James' advice in these times is you must simply pray. He says pain is an invitation to pray and seek God's face. James' recommendation to pray when in pain means you must ask God for healing. Therefore, we see the "ask" element here.

2. Is anyone cheerful?
   Cheerful means happy. So according to James, when you are happy sing psalms. In other words, sing praises. Again, another prayer dimension of praise is revealed. You can read through the verses to see how the other aspects of prayer (as taught by the Lord Jesus) can be practiced.

Now, we can move ahead to the different types of prayers throughout the book. I take this seriously because only knowing we must pray is not enough. Prayer works as a real weapon for unlocking blessings when we pray with knowledge and understanding.

Chapter 3

TYPES OF PRAYERS

I *know it will be* an eye-opening ride but so lovely in the sense it will give you a better understanding of what God expects from you during different times.

Having said that, I first want to give an example of a prayer that has many dimensions to it. Prayer is dynamic. But you don't have to employ all its dynamics in a single prayer. Make time to pray for different things. Pray as you are convicted in your spirit. Definitely pray as you feel the need to seek God for clarity.

Lord, make me an instrument of **thy peace**.
Where there is hatred, **let me sow love**,
Where there is injury, **pardon;**

Where there is doubt, **faith**;
Where there is despair, **hope**;
Where there is darkness, **light;**
And where there is sadness, **joy.**

O Divine Master, grant that I may not so much
seek to be consoled as **to console,**
to be understood as **to understand,**
to be loved, as **to love.**

For it is **in giving** that we receive,
It is **in pardoning** that we are pardoned,
and it is in dying that we **are born to eternal
life.** —St. Francis of Assisi

From the above example, do you see how much
you can say to God? There is so much to pray
about. I highlighted the action words and phrases
to show you the types of prayers you should know:

- The prayer of giving
- The prayer of love
- The prayer of supplication
- The prayer of faith and forgiveness, among
  many

You will read more about these as we explain
in-depth in the book.

Moving ahead, let us take a look at the many types of prayers available to us. Remember, we are speaking of prayer being our ultimate weapon. For the weapon to work properly, you must know how to use it effectively. Unfortunately, you can't successfully make use of something you don't really understand. So, the main aim of this book is to help you comprehend prayer inside out.

> Therefore I exhort first of all that supplications, prayers, intercessions, and giving of thanks be made for all men, for kings and all who are in authority, that we may lead a quiet and peaceable life in all godliness and reverence. For this is good and acceptable in the sight of God our Savior, who desires all men to be saved and to come to the knowledge of the truth. For there is one God and one Mediator between God and men, the Man Christ Jesus, who gave Himself a ransom for all, to be testified in due time, for which I was appointed a preacher and an apostle—I am speaking the truth in Christ and not lying—a teacher of the Gentiles in faith and truth. 1 Timothy 2:1-7, (NKJV)

If there was ever a time we needed prayer, it is now. And as the scripture verse says above, we must position ourselves, not only to pray for our needs but also for others. The gospel was never intended to save only one man—perhaps you. Rather, just like prayer, it was intended for everyone to reap the benefits.

God is calling us to a lifestyle of prayer

In his letter to the church at Ephesus, Paul (from which we derive the theme verses for this book and others in the series) taught them about spiritual warfare. This type of warfare is won in the spiritual realm with prayer knowledge. When you fully have such knowledge, it is easy to pray and win the spiritual battles.

The battle we are speaking about is not against flesh (what we can see and feel) and blood. It is against spiritual forces in high places, which we cannot see with our human eyes.

"For our struggle is not against flesh and blood, but against the rulers, against the authorities, against the powers of this dark world and against the spiritual forces of evil in the heavenly realms" (Ephesians 6:12, NIV).

4 components of demonic activity and the 2 invisible spiritual kingdoms

As we have grown to know (since we are all saved), there are two kingdoms that exist. Both long for your attention—to be able to use you. One uses you for the positive things and good outcomes in your home, society, and nation. However, the other uses you for the complete opposite, which is to inflict pain on you and everyone around you.

I am talking about the kingdom of God and the dominion of Satan, which is under God's kingdom. For the sake of comparison and explanation only, I will refer to Satan's dominion as a kingdom.

These kingdoms operate in the spiritual realm, as widely discussed in the first book of this Trilogy series *Daily Put on the Armor of God "Dress for Spiritual Warfare.*

To discern these two kingdoms and make the right choice, you must be deeply rooted in prayer. Prayer makes a way for you to communicate with the Holy Spirit, who dwells in you once you are saved. If your heart is focused on God's kingdom, you will gravitate toward the things of God.

Below, is the key Scripture verse for this book from different versions of the Bible to reveal its true meaning. It gets interesting this way. Keep

these verses in mind to help you understand what
will unfold as you read further.

Pray in all kinds of prayers – New International Version

> "And pray in the Spirit on all occasions with *all kinds of prayers* and requests. With this in mind, be alert and always keep on praying for all the Lord's people" (Ephesians 6:18, NIV).

Pray in all prayer and supplication – The New King James Versions

> "Praying always with *all prayer and supplication* in the Spirit, being watchful to this end with all perseverance and supplication for all the saints" (Ephesians 6:18, (NKJV).

Pray in the Spirit at all times – The New Living Translation

> "Pray in the Spirit at all times and on every occasion. Stay alert and be persistent in your prayers for all believers everywhere" (Ephesians 6:18, NLT).

The bottom line is we must pray. Ephesians 6:18 is translated differently in each version, but the common theme is we should pray always and in the Spirit.

I will run you through some quick pointers about prayer and what it should look like even before you do it. I want you to get to a point where you think about prayer before going down on your knees, if that is how you pray. Personally, I lay in bed and seek God's face. I pray and talk to God in the shower, in my car, at work, and walking in the park. I want you to get to a point where you reflect on it before saying a single word. And when you think about it, these are the things that are supposed to be in your mind:

1. Prayer is a lifestyle, not an event

You do it every day. There is to be no point where you will tell yourself you have graduated; therefore, you don't need to pray anymore. Even at 90 or 101 years old, you still need to speak to God. Why? It's simple. You are in a relationship with Him, and people in relationships talk to each other.

2. The effective, fervent prayer of a righteous man avails much.

Effective = successful in producing a desired or intended result

Fervent = having or displaying a passionate intensity

Passion doesn't necessarily mean praying loudly or very long. It can be that way sometimes, depending on how the Spirit leads you. Again, I remind you to always pray in the Spirit as I believe Hannah did (1 Samuel 1:10) when the priest thought she was drunk. This happens when the Spirit is the one leading you in prayer.

From Hannah's experience, we see we should not judge people who pray in the Spirit. They may appear be drunk because of their noise and actions but it might not be so. They may be experiencing exactly what the disciples went through on the Day of Pentecost.

Now, I will introduce the various types of prayers in this chapter. However, we will explore them in greater depth later in the book.

The Bible reveals many types of prayers we can use. 1 Timothy 2:1 says,

"First of all, then, I urge that supplications, prayers, intercessions, and thanksgivings be made for all people."

The prayer of request (or supplication)

We must take our requests to God. This emphasizes personal needs. We petition God to supply a need.

"Do not be anxious about anything, but in everything by prayer and supplication with thanksgiving let your requests be made known to God" (Philippians 4:6).

Part of winning the spiritual battle is "praying at all times in the Spirit, with all prayer and supplication."

The prayer of intercession

Many times, our prayers include requests for others as we intercede for them. We are told to make intercession "for everyone." Jesus serves as our example in this area. The entire chapter of John 17 is a prayer from Jesus on behalf of His disciples and all believers.

Christ begins by praying for Himself. This, along with His example of prayer also recorded in

Scripture (Matthew 6:9–13) proves it is reasonable to pray on our own behalf. The primary purpose of this is asking for God's will to be done; this is always for His glory (John 17:1) and our ultimate benefit (Romans 8:28–30). At this moment, Jesus notes "the hour" has finally arrived for His sacrifice on behalf of mankind (John 3:16; 12:32–33). The means by which mankind can access eternal life is about to be fulfilled (John 17:1–5).

Next, Jesus prays for His followers. In the most immediate context, these prayers are for the apostles (Matthew 10:1–4). The men personally trained by Jesus will experience massive resistance as they preach His truth. However, it is their teaching that will lead others to faith in Christ (John 17:20).

The prayer of thanksgiving

The attitude of gratitude—we see another type of prayer in Philippians 4:6: thanksgiving or thanks to God.

> "With thanksgiving let your requests
> be made known to God."

Many examples of thanksgiving prayers can be found in the psalms. We praise God for what He has done.

The prayer of agreement (also known as corporate prayer)

After Jesus' ascension, the disciples "all joined together constantly in prayer" (Acts 1:14).

> Then they returned to Jerusalem from the mount called Olivet, which is near Jerusalem, a Sabbath day's journey. And when they had entered, they went up into the upper room where they were staying: Peter, James, John, and Andrew; Philip and Thomas; Bartholomew and Matthew; James the son of Alphaeus and Simon the Zealot; and Judas the son of James. These all continued with one accord in prayer and supplication, with the women and Mary the mother of Jesus, and with His brothers.
>
> (Acts 1:12-14)

After Pentecost, the early church "devoted themselves" to prayer (Acts 2:42). Their example encourages us to pray with others.

The prayer of worship

The prayer of worship is similar to the prayer of thanksgiving. The difference is that worship focuses on who God is, whereas thanksgiving focuses on what God has done.

The prayer of consecration

Sometimes, prayer is a time of setting ourselves apart to follow God's will. Jesus made such a prayer the night before His crucifixion:

> "And going a little farther he fell on his face and prayed, saying, 'My Father, if it be possible, let this cup pass from me; nevertheless, not as I will, but as you will'" (Matthew 26:39).

The Prayer in the Garden

> Then Jesus came with them to a place called Gethsemane, and said to the disciples, "Sit here while I go and pray over there." **And He took with Him Peter and the two sons of Zebedee, and He began to be sorrowful and deeply distressed.** Then He said to them, "My soul is exceedingly sorrowful, even to death. Stay here and watch with Me." **He**

went a little farther and fell on His face, and prayed, saying, "O My Father, if it is possible, let this cup pass from Me; nevertheless, not as I will, but as You will." Then He came to the disciples and found them sleeping, and said to Peter, "What! Could you not watch with Me one hour? **Watch and pray, lest you enter into temptation. The spirit indeed is willing, but the flesh is weak."** Again, a second time, He went away and prayed, saying, "O My Father, [a]if this cup cannot pass away from Me unless I drink it, Your will be done." **And He came and found them asleep again, for their eyes were heavy.** So He left them, went away again, and prayed the third time, saying the same words. **Then He came to His disciples and said to them, "Are you still sleeping and resting? Behold, the hour [b] is at hand, and the Son of Man is being betrayed into the hands of sinners.** Rise, let us be going. See, My betrayer is at hand." (Matthew 26:36-46, NKJV, emphasis mine)

PRAYING IN THE SPIRIT

For if I pray in a tongue, my spirit prays, but my understanding is unfruitful. What is the conclusion then? I will pray with the spirit, and I will also pray with the understanding. I will sing with the spirit, and I will also sing with the understanding. (1 Corinthians 14:14-15, NKJV)

IN THE SPIRIT = NOT IN THE FLESH

Prayer in the spirit is fervent, faith-filled, word-based communication with God.

Prayer is having a conversation with God and should be made without ceasing. As we grow in our love for Jesus Christ, we will naturally desire to talk to Him.

Prayer is mandatory for spiritual progress. It is not optional. I want you to hold on to these words as we begin to unpack each type of prayer in the coming chapters.

Chapter 4

A Prayer of Worship

In this chapter, we will learn more about the prayer of worship. Below are verses from the Bible that give us examples of how the prayer of worship sounds. Note this type of prayer does not have to include requests for anything from God. Rather, it speaks about who God is, what He has done for us, and what He can do for us for eternity. A prayer of worship is not asking for things from God but about loving Him for who He is.

> Sing to the LORD, all the earth; proclaim his salvation day after day. Declare his glory among the nations, his marvelous deeds among all peoples.

For great is the LORD and most worthy of praise; he is to be feared above all gods. For all the gods of the nations are idols, but the LORD made the heavens. Splendor and majesty are before him; strength and joy are in his dwelling place. Ascribe to the LORD, all you families of nations, ascribe to the LORD glory and strength. Ascribe to the LORD the glory due his name; bring an offering and come before him. Worship the LORD in the splendor of his holiness. Tremble before him, all the earth! The world is firmly established; it cannot be moved. Let the heavens rejoice, let the earth be glad; let them say among the nations, "The LORD reigns!"

(1 Chronicles 16:23-31)

To be clear, praying to God and worshiping Him are not about the deed itself. It should be done in Spirit and in truth. In other words, seek first to be in Spirit. Get the connection with God in Spirit and then enjoy the worship.

"God is spirit, and his worshipers must worship in the Spirit and in truth" (John 4:24, NIV).

Worshiping God in Spirit goes hand in hand with doing so in truth as well. The above verse first mentions the Spirit and later on "truth" in the same sentence. By observation, you notice that the word "Spirit" is written with a capital "S," in reference to the Holy Spirit, a person. Below are verses of Scripture about the Spirit.

"God is spirit" (John 4:24a, NIV).

Here, it is revealed to us God is Spirit. He is not made of flesh like humans. For this reason, you are asked, in the same verse, to worship Him in Spirit and in truth. Truth is mentioned as a way of revealing God is the truth, the way, and the life. The truth is the Word of God; anything contrary is a lie.

Therefore, when speaking to God, our Father in heaven, first connect with Him in Spirit. This must come from a point of truth and our lives must be truthful, not falling for the lies of the Enemy.

Remember, we are still speaking about prayer being the ultimate weapon. It is important to know prayer is done in the spirit. The type of prayer that is called worship has the power to unlock many blessings for you, even if you have not asked for them. I will give a few examples from the Bible after this, just to show you how much God does when His people worship Him.

You can worship God in everything you do. When you clean your house, do it unto the Lord. When you go to work, do it unto the Lord. When you exercise, do it unto the Lord.

"The earth was formless and void, and darkness was over the surface of the deep, and the **Spirit of God** was moving over the surface of the waters" (Genesis 1:2).

Then the angel who was speaking with me returned and roused me, as a man who is awakened from his sleep. He said to me, "What do you see?" And I said, "I see, and behold, a lampstand all of gold with its bowl on the top of it, and its seven lamps on it with seven spouts belonging to each of the lamps which are on the top of it; also two olive trees by it, one on the right side of the bowl and the other on its left side." Then I said to the angel who was speaking with me saying, "What are these, my lord?" So the angel who was speaking with me answered and said to me, "Do you not know what these are?"

And I said, "No, my lord." Then he said to me, "This is the word of the Lord to Zerubbabel saying, 'Not by might nor by power, but by **My Spirit**,' says the Lord of hosts. 'What are you, O Great Mountain? Before Zerubbabel you will become a plain; and he will bring forth the top stone with shouts of "Grace, grace to it!"'" (Zechariah 4:1-7)

Not only did I want to show you God is Spirit, but I also want to reveal to you His spirit lives in us. He lives with us all the time. And, when we yield to Him (turn our hearts toward God and His will), there is no mountain too big for Him to move.

It reminds me of a certain song, which says,

> There's no shadow You won't light up
> Mountain You won't climb up
> Coming after me
> There's no wall You won't kick down
> Lie You won't tear down
> Coming after me.
> (Cory Ashby, "Reckless Love")

Worship God, and worship Him alone. Worship is another form of prayer. It is powerful! Make use of this as an ultimate weapon for spiritual warfare.

"And when you pray, do not babble on like pagans, for they think that by their many words they will be heard. Do not be like them, for your Father knows what you need before you ask Him"

(Matthew 6:7-8, NIV).

Scripture teaches us God already knows what we desire even before we pray; these words came directly from Jesus Christ to us. As such, it is possible that, sometimes, you don't know what you really need or want from God when praying. You may miss many things that you could have asked from God. Under such circumstances, what you do is worship Him. Pray in your heavenly language (if you don't have a heavenly language ask God to give you one). I teach on the subject of speaking in tongues in my book *The Person with Power, the Holy Spirit Dwelling on the Inside.* Sit in His presence and seek His wisdom.

When you worship God in Spirit and in truth, it becomes a weapon for winning.

Praise the LORD.
Praise God in his sanctuary;
praise him in his mighty heavens.

*Praise him **for his acts of power**;*
*praise him **for his surpassing greatness**.*
*Praise him **with the sounding of the trumpet**,*
*praise him **with the harp and lyre**,*
*praise him **with tambourine and dancing**,*
*praise him **with the strings and flute**,*
*praise **him with the clash of cymbals**,*
*praise **him with resounding cymbals**.*
Let everything that has breath praise the LORD.
Praise the LORD. (Psalm 150:1-6, emphasis mine)

The same weapons or instruments being used for praising God can be used to worship Him.

In this psalm, it seems as if David is writing about praising God but with strong connotations of worship. You see this here, *"Praise him **for his acts of power**; praise him **for his surpassing greatness**."*

When you praise God for His greatness, you are doing so for who He is, even if He hasn't done anything for you yet; you just know He can do it. That is worship. But when you praise Him after the fact, when He has done something already, it is praise.

Trumpets can also be used as instruments of worship as seen below in the following Scripture passage.

Now the gates of Jericho were securely barred because of the Israelites. No one went out and no one came in.

Then the Lord said to Joshua, "See, I have delivered Jericho into your hands, along with its king and its fighting men. March around the city once with all the armed men. Do this for six days. Have seven priests carry trumpets of rams' horns in front of the ark. On the seventh day, march around the city seven times, with the priests blowing the trumpets. When you hear them sound a long blast on the trumpets, have the whole army give a loud shout; then the wall of the city will collapse and the army will go up, everyone straight in."

So Joshua son of Nun called the priests and said to them, "Take up the ark of the covenant of the Lord and have seven priests carry trumpets in front of it." And he ordered the army, "Advance! March around the city, with an armed guard going ahead of the ark of the Lord."

When Joshua had spoken to the people, the seven priests carrying the seven trumpets before the Lord went forward, **blowing their trumpets**, and **the ark of the Lord's covenant followed them**. The armed guard marched ahead of the priests who blew the trumpets, and the rear guard followed the ark. All this time the trumpets were sounding. But Joshua had commanded the army, "Do not give a war cry, do not raise your voices, do not say a word until the day I tell you to shout. Then shout!" So he had the ark of the Lord carried around the city, circling it once. Then the army returned to camp and spent the night there.

Joshua got up early the next morning and the priests took up the ark of the Lord. The seven priests carrying the seven trumpets went forward, marching before the ark of the Lord and blowing the trumpets. The armed men went ahead of them and the rear guard followed the ark of the Lord, while the trumpets kept sounding. So on the second day they marched around the city once and returned to the camp. They did this for six days.

On the seventh day, they got up at daybreak and marched around the city seven times in the same manner, except that on that day they circled the city seven times. The seventh time around, when the priests sounded the trumpet blast, Joshua commanded the army, **"Shout! For the Lord has given you the city!** The city and all that is in it are to be devoted to the Lord. Only Rahab the prostitute and all who are with her in her house shall be spared, because she hid the spies we sent. But keep away from the devoted things, so that you will not bring about your own destruction by taking any of them. Otherwise you will make the camp of Israel liable to destruction and bring trouble on it. All the silver and gold and the articles of bronze and iron are sacred to the Lord and must go into his treasury."

When the trumpets sounded, the army shouted, and at the sound of the trumpet, when the men gave a loud shout, the wall collapsed; so everyone charged straight in, and they took the city. They devoted the city to the Lord and destroyed with the sword every living thing in it—men and women, young and old, cattle, sheep and donkeys.

(Joshua 6:1-20, emphasis mine)

The priests blowing the seven trumpets and the Ark of the Covenant following behind them was a sign that when you worship God, His presence comes with you. Moreover, when it does, there are always results to look forward to.

In verse 16, Joshua commands his people to shout because the Lord has given them the city, which on its own is interesting since He had confirmed the city was given to them before they actually shouted.

The point is you should shout and worship God in advance. Once you do that, His presence comes to you as symbolized by the Ark of the Covenant, which followed the priests all the way. And, when His presence comes down, your own version of the walls of Jericho will come crashing down. You will walk freely without having to lift a finger.

Life becomes peaceful when you worship God. When you lift your voice, God will move heaven and earth on your behalf. It requires less energy and strength from you but you get more joy and victory. Use the prayer of worship as your ultimate weapon and expect God to work on your behalf.

God delivered the children of Israel under King Jehoshaphat when they worshipped Him while facing war against the Moabites and their allies. Read 2 Chronicles Chapter 20.

How You Can Worship God
Kneeling Down

For he will deliver the needy who cry out,
the afflicted who have no one to help.
He will take pity on the weak and the needy

and save the needy from death.
He will rescue them from oppression and violence,
for precious is their blood in his sight.
Long may he live!
May gold from Sheba be given him.
May people ever pray for him
and bless him all day long. (Psalm 72:12-15)

To kneel down is to bless God. You bow down to Him. This way of worship is known as *barak*, which means to bow down to or kneel before the Lord.

You bow down in acknowledgment of how great God is, how much He deserves to be recognized as the almighty. Doing this is also not from a begging point of view. Rather, you are in a state of expectation when you speak to God this way because you know He is your Father who listens when you speak to Him.

You boast in His presence

The Hebrew word called *halal* means you are vibrant; you are shining; you are boasting and celebrating how good God is. Remember when speaking about the story of Joshua, we mentioned you can boast (worship) God even before He delivers what you are expecting in prayer. This boasting is backed by the fact you trust in God's abilities.

> "David appointed the following Levites to lead the people in worship before the Ark of the Lord—to invoke his blessings, to give thanks, and to praise the Lord, the God of Israel" (1 Chronicles 16:4).

This kind of worship is said to appear more than 110 times in the Old Testament alone. It is translated as "to shine, boast, rave about, celebrate or even to be vociferously foolish." Can you imagine a more wondrous noise raving about everything the Lord is and all He has done?

You can shout out loud

This type of worship is called *shabach.*

> "Shout joyfully to the Lord, all the earth; Break forth and sing for joy and sing praises"
> (Psalm 98:4).

This kind of shouting is loud and commanding. As such, no worshipper of God does so while feeling sorry for himself. Shabach houses all the traits of confidence in God. A person doing this is not afraid to make noise and is definitely not afraid people will think he has gone mad. He is not concerned over what they will say about the God he is making noise to who does not answer aloud.

I say this because many people have limited the way they worship God because of the fear of what others will say if tomorrow it all seems not to be working. Well, for people like this, I only have one sentence: God remains the same, yesterday, today, and forever. He is not changed by circumstances as humans are.

You can sing Him praises

This type of worship is called *tehillah,* which means to sing praises. When singing these praises, you do it out of the spirit spontaneously. As we have already mentioned, God must be worshipped in Spirit and in truth.

> Oh come, let us sing to the Lord; let us make a joyful noise to the rock of our salvation!
>
> Let us come into his presence with thanksgiving; let us make a joyful noise to him with songs of praise!

> For the Lord is a great God and a great King above all gods.
>
> In his hand are the depths of the earth; the heights of the mountains are his also. The sea is his, for he made it, and his hands formed the dry land. (Psalm 95:1-5)

Singing praises to God is usually spontaneous. It is unplanned and unrehearsed but only comes from your heart.

You can raise your hands

This becomes interesting, especially considering what we spoke about before—that when you worship God, it becomes a weapon to solving your problems. Below is another example of this from the Bible:

> The Amalekites came and attacked the Israelites at Rephidim. Moses said to Joshua, "Choose some of our men and go out to fight the Amalekites. Tomorrow I will stand on top of the hill with the staff of God in my hands." So Joshua fought the Amalekites as Moses had ordered, and Moses, Aaron and Hur went to the top of the hill. As long as Moses held up

his hands, the Israelites were winning, but whenever he lowered his hands, the Amalekites were winning. When Moses' hands grew tired, they took a stone and put it under him and he sat on it. Aaron and Hur held his hands up—one on one side, one on the other—so that his hands remained steady till sunset. So Joshua overcame the Amalekite army with the sword. (Exodus 17:8-13, NIV)

Here, we see Moses being in a position where he is lifting up his hands, resulting in the Israelites winning in their war. But when his hands were lowered, they would get a beating from the Amalekites who had come to attack them.

Now, from this action, we see Moses' hands as a sign of worship to God, even as a sign of surrendering to God's will. It unlocks God's presence among them and causes them to win the battle.

This kind of worship is called *towpath,* which is done through the extending of hands. As you do this, you express thanks for what God has done or will do for you. Remember, you are saying God can do all the things I desire.

"But giving thanks is a sacrifice that truly honors me. If you keep to my path, I will reveal to you the salvation of God" (Psalm 50:23).

Play music for God

The last type of worship I will share with you is called *zamar*, which means to touch the strings of an instrument, thus making music with instruments and mostly rejoicing for God.

Praise him with a blast of the ram's horn; praise him with the lyre and harp! Praise him with the tambourine and dancing; praise him with strings and flutes! Praise him with a clash of cymbals; praise him with loud clanging cymbals. Let everything that breathes sing praises to the Lord! Praise the Lord!
(Psalm 150:3-6)

You can still worship God this way if you can't play any instrument. You can clap your hands. They are instruments of praise and worship. Use them!

Chapter 5

BEING WATCHFUL TO THIS END

"Praying always with all prayer and supplication in the Spirit, being watchful to this end with all perseverance and supplication for all the saints" (Ephesians 6:18).

I n this chapter, we shall talk about being watchful to this end. However, let us review some of the points we already talked about in the previous chapters.

In the first part of this series, we said our motives are central in our prayers. When praying, it doesn't matter what your words or utterances are. What matters is what is in your heart. Those are your motives. Your motives will determine how you pray. Scriptures teach those who pray with improper motives have their reward already (Matthew 6:1-8; James 4:3).

We also said we don't have to pray aloud, and we don't have to pray long unless specifically directed by the Holy Spirit. You are always in prayer mode and praying mood 247/365 regardless of what you may be doing at that moment (I Thessalonians 5:17).

You may be on your way to work; you are praying. You are on your way to school; you are praying. You are in a conversation or a conference; you are praying under your breath. It covers every aspect of our lives. Praying without ceasing means you can pray every moment of your breathing life. It doesn't have to be loud or long.

Can you see your prayer is like your breath? Praying is like breathing. The pulse rate of the heartbeat is not loud and long but yet continuous. When somebody ceases to breathe, you know what happens. Likewise, when we cease to pray as Christians, it attracts an emergency situation. Just as we always breathe to be alive in our bodies, God wants us to always pray to be alive both in our spirits and bodies.

We talked about the "Prayer of Request" (or supplication). We discovered we are to take our requests to God on our behalf or on behalf of somebody else. This emphasizes the person needs to petition for God to supply a need. A brilliant scriptural illustration is (Daniel Chapter 9) when Daniel made supplication for himself and his country.

Then, we talked about "Prayer of Intercession." This is when you pray to intercede on behalf of somebody. You can intercede for your spouse, children, friends, family, parents, and loved ones. You can also intercede for your work, business, and country. Remember when Daniel prayed (Daniel Chapter 9). Daniel was interceding for his country.

Our brilliant sister, Esther, when Haman had perfected his plan to destroy the Jews, Esther made up her mind to meet her husband king Ahasuerus uninvited, which usually attracted the death penalty. Nonetheless, Esther chose the path of death to save her people. But she asked her people to intercede on her behalf (Esther 4:16).

In the New Testament, Acts 12:1-12, to be precise, when Herod the king killed James the brother of John and saw the Jews were pleased, he got Peter arrested, so he could kill him as well. However, the church interceded for him.

Finally, for the Christians, the Scriptures teach the Holy Spirit intercedes for us (Romans 8:26) and in 1 John 2:1 Jesus Christ is with the Father advocating for us.

We talked about the "Prayer of Thanksgiving." Thanksgiving, we said, is an attitude of gratitude. Philippians 4:6 says, "Be anxious for nothing, but in everything by prayer and supplication, with thanksgiving, let your requests be made known to God."

The next one we talked about was the "Prayer of Agreement." The prayer of agreement is when we come together either in groups, corporate prayer, and worship praying for needs. Two or more individuals involved in the prayer must be in agreement. Recall the Scriptures say, "Where two or three are gathered together in my name, there am I in their midst" (Matthew 18:20).

We also know one can send a thousand away and two can put ten thousand to flight (Deuteronomy 32:20). When we come together in agreement, we accomplish more for the kingdom of God.

We also talked about the "Prayer of Worship." The prayer of worship is similar to the prayer of thanksgiving but with a little variation. Prayers of worship focus on who God is, whereas prayers of thanksgiving focus on what God has done. We know who God is.

Who God Is!

- I Am That I Am (Exodus 3:14)
- Our Redeemer (Galatians 3:13)
- The Ancient of Days (Daniel 7:9)
- The God Almighty (Genesis 48:15)
- The Bishop of My Soul (1 Peter 2:25)
- The Chief Cornerstone (Ephesians 2:20)
- The First and the Last (Revelation 22:13)
- The Shepherd of My Soul (1 Peter 2:25)
- He is the Alpha and Omega (Revelation 1:8)
- The Rose of Sharon (Song of Solomon 2:1)
- The Lily of the Valley (Song of Solomon 2:1)
- The Beginning and the End (Revelation 22:13)
- The Bright and Morning Star (Revelation 22:16)

What God has done

- He saved you
- He gave hope
- He redeemed you
- He saved your children

- He regulated your mind
- He healed your body
- He healed your finances
- He gave a new life and new beginning
- He brought you out of darkness into His marvelous light

Has God done something for you?

Thereafter, we talked about the "Prayer of Consecration." We saw when Jesus Christ was in the garden of Gethsemane (Matthew 26:36-46) praying to God about His death on the cross. He asked God to take the cup from Him. Nonetheless, He acknowledges under the circumstance, it was not His will but the will of God that counts. Thus, in obedience, He consecrated Himself submitting to God's will.

Sometimes in our Christian journey we come to that junction and the direction, though obvious, seems too horrendous for us. At these times, do as Jesus Christ did. Consecrate yourself to God. Inevitably, you will come across times in your life when you don't know what to do or where to go. Beloved, then, you must consecrate yourself to God and submit to His will. Be quiet inside and do what God asks you to do.

The last thing we talked about is "Supplication in the Spirit." That is the power of prayer. It is praying in the Spirit. Let me give you the definition of praying in the Spirit as the Father gave it to me. "Praying in the Spirit is simply not praying in the flesh."

I already gave you a working definition of what that is. But, let me give it here again. Praying in the Spirit is fervent faith-filled word-based communication with God. "God is a Spirit: and they that worship him must worship him in spirit and in truth" (John 4:24). As a continuation, we talked about supplication for all saints. That is the prayer of petition. Having said that, let us go into the subject of this chapter.

Being Watchful to the End with Perseverance

For clarity, let's redefine "watchful" in this context as "prudence." What does "prudence" mean? "Prudence" means being cautious. Therefore, being watchful to the end means not fainting or giving up. It doesn't matter what it looks like, you will be watchful to the end. You will persevere until the answer comes. You will be faithful and vigilant until you see or have the manifestation of what it is you are seeking God for.

Don't fall asleep on what you are asking or seeking God for. Look attentively to Him with the expectation He will respond to what you prayed for. Yes, it may not look like anything close to your expectation, but the witness and conviction are in you that your desire and request will be delivered.

Delay doesn't mean denial. Even though you don't have it right now, it doesn't mean you will not have it. Draw some strength and counsel from Abraham and Sarah's approach as they waited for Isaac:

> And being not weak in faith, he considered not his own body now dead, when he was about an hundred years old, neither yet the deadness of Sarah's womb: He staggered not at the promise of God through unbelief; but was strong in faith, giving glory to God; And being fully persuaded that, what he had promised, he was able also to perform. And therefore it was imputed to him for righteousness. Now it was not written for his sake alone, that it was imputed to him; But for us also, to whom it shall be imputed, if we believe on him that raised up Jesus our Lord from the dead; Who was delivered for our offences, and was raised again for our justification. (Romans 4:19-25)

Being Watchful to the End Means I Am in Expectation!

Let's examine this familiar example. Assuming I don't have food or any money to shop for food, I pray, asking God to send me some food. Being watchful to the end means the next thing I will do after praying for food is to set the table with the expectation God will provide.

I am hopeful and know God will do something. But I don't know when, and I don't know how. Still, I am persuaded He will intervene and food is coming. Your attitude is as if the food has already arrived. After you have set the table and asked, "Lord, where is the food?" Right there, you hear a knock on your door and somebody shows up. "I was at the grocery store today and the Lord asked me to get this for you. It sounds crazy to me. I didn't know what I was doing getting groceries I have no need off, but I was obeying whatever it is the Lord wants me to do."

That is how to be watchful to the end. It means trusting completely God will do what He said He will do. Thus, you have a role to play. You may be God's answer to somebody's need or prayer. Don't try to rationalize to make sense out of it. As long as you are obedient, God is pleased.

In summary, being watchful to the end means we have to put on the attitude of expectation. We must be watchful to the end knowing God will provide. We must operate out of the spirit of expectation. Now, the big question is, what are you expecting?

The following story is about the congregation in a small village. The accounts are different but the idea remains the same. The village was a small farming community that was experiencing drought and famine. The pastor of the congregation called a prayer meeting to pray God would send some rain. Every day, the congregation gathered to pray. They prayed for days; still, there was no rain. One day, a nine-year-old boy went outside with his umbrella in the open space and prayed God would send rain.

Not long after he finished praying, it started to rain. The lesson in this short story is the little boy expected God would answer his prayer for rain. So he brought his umbrella with him. On the contrary, the villagers or the congregation, including the pastor who called the prayer service, though earnestly praying with a good deal of sincerity, seemed not to expect God would send the rain.

This story brings to mind the disciples' attitude when they interceded for Peter who was to be killed by King Herod (Acts Chapter 12). God heard their prayers and Peter was delivered. But when Peter arrived at the house where the disciples were praying and knocked, a little girl named Rhoda ran to the door. On hearing Peter's voice, instead of opening the door, she ran back in excitement to the disciples telling them Peter was at the door (Acts 12:14).

The disciples kept praying saying she was mad (Acts 12:15). She insisted Peter was at the door knocking. Then the disciples told her it was his angel (Acts 12:15b). Peter kept knocking at the door. Perhaps, Peter's knocking and the distraction from the girl got unbearable and they finally opened the door. To their astonishment, Peter was standing before them (Acts 12:16). Note, even the disciples didn't pray in expectation. Here is the scriptural reference:

Now about that time Herod the king stretched forth his hands to vex certain of the church. And he killed James the brother of John with the sword. And because he saw it pleased the Jews, he proceeded further to take Peter also. (Then were the days of unleavened bread.) And when he had apprehended him, he put him in prison, and delivered him to four quaternions of soldiers to keep him; intending after Easter to bring him forth to the people. Peter therefore was kept in prison: but prayer was made without ceasing of the church unto God for him

(Acts 12:1-5)

And when he had considered the thing, he came to the house of Mary the mother of John, whose surname was Mark; where many were gathered together praying. And as Peter knocked at the door of the gate, a damsel came to hearken, named Rhoda. And when she knew Peter's voice, she opened not the gate for gladness, but ran in, and told how Peter stood before the gate. And they said unto her, Thou art mad. But she constantly affirmed that it was even so. Then said they, It is his angel. But Peter continued knocking: and when they had opened the door, and saw him, they were astonished. But he, beckoning unto them with the hand to hold their peace, declared unto them how the Lord had brought him out of the prison. And he said, Go shew these things unto James, and to the brethren. And he departed, and went into another place.

(Acts 12:12-17)

Expect What You Pray For!

The day my husband Greg and I came back from our honeymoon, we needed $100 dollars. My husband was really in need of this money. I was confident God would provide. We didn't know how He was going to do it, but we knew He would provide. Having been away for some time, we went to my office and looked through my mail.

We took them into the car and I started opening them one after the other. As I opened one of the envelopes there was a check for $100 dollars. Did God truly provide? Yes, He did. We didn't know how He was going to do it; we didn't know when He was going to do it, and we didn't know where He was going to do it. But He provided.

God can accomplish everything He promised you. Ephesian 3:20 says God can do exceedingly, abundantly above all we ask or think, according to the power that works in us. The power that works in us is the Holy Spirit. We must yield to Him always because that is how our needs are supplied. In addition, remember God blesses us continuously so we can bless others continuously.

Bread and Fish Dinner

Being watchful to the end entails being blessings to others. God wants to use somebody else to be a blessing to you. Before Jesus Christ performed the miracle of feeding the five thousand, He told His disciples to give them something to eat. But Philip said, "Lord, we have nothing to offer them as dinner."

However, a little boy with his lunch pack was in the crowd. Of course, five loaves and two fishes were not enough to feed five thousand people. So the disciples complained about the quantity. What were five loaves and two fishes compared to the size of the famished crowd? Jesus Christ said let me have the bread and fish and instructed the people should be made to sit down for a meal.

The first thing Jesus Christ did when He received the bread and fish was to lift them to heaven to the God of multiplication and He prayed, giving Him thanks. After He prayed, He started breaking and sharing the bread and fish dinner. Everyone had enough and twelve baskets were left over.

This proves no matter how small, God can accomplish His purpose when we yield to Him. The little you have and think is not enough is more than enough for you. It can actually feed the nation.

Prayer Is Mandatory, Not Optional

As we saw in the fish dinner, Jesus Christ had to say a prayer of thanksgiving first before breaking and sharing the bread and fish. That demonstrates the importance of prayer. In this circumstance, considering the crowd and the size of the dinner, prayer was needed; otherwise, the bread and fish wouldn't have multiplied.

Let me quickly say you cannot lack to the extent you and your family are starving. This is true because Jesus Christ proved it and has shown you what to do when you don't have enough. All you require is to yield to the God of increase giving Him thanks for the little you have.

We must understand, for spiritual development, growth, and spiritual warfare, prayer is essential. For a victorious Christian life, prayer and praying are binding and not discretionary.

Prayer Demonstrates Your Relationship with God

Prayer is you communicating with God in conversation. It is a function of your relationship with God. Can you imagine being in a relationship where there are no conversations? What kind of relationship would that be? This was the case of Eli and Samuel (1 Samuel Chapter 3). It is very risky as you can see from the Scriptures. Imagine a prophet and priest who cannot recognize the voice of God. Samuel was young at the time when he did not recognize God's voice; it meant there was no relationship. If I am in a relationship with you, and I am not talking to you, then we are not really in a relationship. Are we? When you are in a relationship with someone and the person calls your name, you recognize the voice.

That is how our relationship with God should be. When you cannot hear or recognize the voice of God, it demonstrates your relationship with Him is broken and perhaps, His displeasure. So, examine your life and repent. When we disobey God, our relationship with Him ends. It happened to Eli the prophet. King Saul was also a victim.

In Acts Chapter 12, the disciples came together praying for Peter. Once Rhoda the little girl heard the knock on the door, she ran to open it. Before she could do so, she heard Peter's voice. Recognizing Peter's voice, she ran back in joy and left the door unopened. How did she recognize Peter's voice? She was in a relationship with Peter.

Since she had a relationship with Peter, she was waiting in expectation. Because she was waiting in expectation she was eager and ran to the door when she heard the knock. She was in an agape relationship, a Christian family relationship of love.

God wants us to be in an intimate relationship with Him. So, when the Enemy comes pretending as he did in the garden of Eden (Genesis Chapter 3), you will know it is not God's voice. Jesus Christ corroborates this in John Chapter 10, when He said my sheep know my voice and the voice of a stranger they will not follow (John 10:1-5 & 27).

When your inner voice is speaking to you, you know it is not God's voice. But, when you hear God's voice, you are quick to respond because you know it.

Having recognized prayer is communication or conversation with God, let us examine the "Lord's Prayer" as was taught by Jesus Christ.

The "Lord's Prayer" (Mathew 6:9-13)

When Jesus Christ was with the disciples, He performed several miracles. He opened blind eyes, healed the sick, raised the dead, calmed the sea, and walked upon the water. He healed the crippled man, the lady who had an issue of blood for twelve years, and fed over five thousand with a kid's lunch pack of five loaves of bread and two fishes. But, when Jesus was about to go back to God, the disciples did something interesting. They said to Jesus Christ, "Lord, teach us how to pray."

This request is instructive and touching because they didn't say teach us how to perform miracles. They didn't say teach us how to lay hands on somebody and transfer the Holy Spirit or the anointing. They said Lord, teach us how to pray. Nowhere in the Scriptures did Jesus Christ pray with His disciples, so this request was like that of King Solomon's for wisdom. 1 Kings 3:1-15 demonstrates the earnestness and rectitude of their hearts.

Jesus Christ was always going to quiet places to pray alone except when He went to pray on the Mount of Gethsemane. Though He had all the disciples there with Him, He only took Peter, James, and John with Him to pray (Matthew 26:36-46). Even then, He kept some distance between Him and them. He went alone to pray to His Father.

The Model of Prayer

Now let us look at the model of prayer Jesus Christ gave His disciples.

Pray is an Acronym of Praise, Repent, Ask, and Yield

Jesus Christ taught His disciples how to pray by giving them the following prayer model.

In this manner, therefore, pray:
Our Father in heaven,
Hallowed be Your name.
Your kingdom come.
Your will be done
On earth as it is in heaven.
Give us this day our daily bread.
And forgive us our debts,
As we forgive our debtors.
And do not lead us into temptation,
But deliver us from the evil one.
[a]For Yours is the kingdom and the power and the
glory forever. Amen. (Mathew 6:9-13)

We call it the "Lord's Prayer." The Lord's Prayer is a foundation for prayer. It is a blueprint of how to pray. It has four key points in it that we focus on whenever we pray. These points are praise, repent, ask, and yield. Thus, P-R-A-Y is an acronym of praise, repent, ask, and yield.

Praise

> Hallowed be the Name of our Father in heaven; for thine is the kingdom, and the power and the glory, forever.

The first key we learn from this prayer model is praise. This model teaches when we pray to God the first thing we do is to praise Him and give Him thanks. This was seen when Jesus Christ fed the five thousand (John 6:1-14). You must praise God for who He is, and what He has made manifest in your lives. Some things we can praise God for are His mercy, great things in our lives, and forgiving us of our sins. We praise God because Jesus Christ was obedient unto the death on the cross of Calvary. We ultimately praise God because He is praiseworthy. You don't praise God because you feel like it. You praise God because it is an instruction. We praise God in Spirit and in truth.

The truth is God is merciful and His love endures forever. So, praise Him. To access God, you need praise and thanksgiving.

> Make a joyful shout to the Lord, all you lands!
> Serve the Lord with gladness;

Come before His presence with singing.
Know that the Lord, He is God;
It is He who has made us, and not we ourselves;
We are His people and the sheep of His pasture.
Enter into His gates with thanksgiving,
And into His courts with praise.
Be thankful to Him, and bless His name.
For the Lord is good;
His mercy is everlasting,
And His truth endures to all generations.
(Psalm 100: 1-4)

The Scripture passage above teaches us to enter God's gates with thanksgiving and His courts with praise. It didn't say if or when you feel like it. It didn't say if and when everything is lining up. It didn't say if and when everything is working out. It didn't say if and when you are happy.

As Christians, the joy of the Lord is our strength. It does not matter if we are happy or not; we must praise God. If we praise God because we are happy, we are saying our praise to Him depends on the mood. So, quit singing songs like "If you are happy and you know it, clap your hands."

If you are happy and know or if you are not happy and you know, you must still clap your hands because the joy of the Lord is your strength (Nehemiah 8:10) and His love is shed abroad in your heart by the Holy Spirit who lives inside of you (Romans 5:5).

Understand that if "happiness depends on your happenings," when your happenings are not right, your joy evaporates. This is one of the reasons people are depressed. The source of their joy or happiness is external, man-made, and transitory.

Repent

> Forgive us our sins, as we forgive those who sin against us.

Two Aspects of Our Imagination

The two aspects of our imaginations are namely, the sanctified imagination and vain imagination (2 Corinthians 10:5).

Vain imagination is imagining, magnifying, or meditating on negative thoughts. On the contrary, sanctified imagination, is imagining, magnifying, or dwelling on positive thoughts. Apostle Paul says whatsoever is of good report meditate on these things (Philippians 4:8).

Vain imagination is the world's system of thinking. An example is "I am never going to make it." "I am a bad parent." It means spending time thinking of things of the world. It also means the dreadful thought that something sinister or negative is going to happen.

You can recognize vain imaginations with words like

- I wish I could
- I can't make it
- If I only had
- What, If I did not

They include these three:

- The lust of the eyes
- The lust of the flesh
- The pride of life

Everything your eyes see you want to have. I want to have this. I want to have that, and I want to have it all. It is covetousness (Luke 12:15-20; 1John 2:15-17). A vain imagination is glazed in greed, fear, anxiety, doubts, and impossibilities. In summary, it is developed from the heart of unbelief or the uncircumcised heart. Therefore, guard your heart with all diligence for out of it are the issues of life (Proverbs 4:23). As believers, we have sanctified imaginations, the function of the mind of Christ (1 Corinthians 2:16).

It means screening the events of your life through the Word of God. It means your thoughts, language, communications, and conversations are synchronized with the Word of God (Matthew 12:34-37; Luke 6:45). The sanctified imagination develops from the circumcised heart.

Recognize though the tendencies are there as we go about our daily chores, we should never get stuck in vain imaginations. For instance, an individual has a premonition of a disaster or some kind of evil. The vain imagination will stop there without doing anything. At worst, it goes about spilling the negative thought poisoning every environment and mind that cares to listen.

Contrarily, the sanctified imagination, knowing about the impending doom, will seek solutions by examining the Word of God, praying and seeking the face of God about the situation—being watchful to the end that God will intervene.

Yes, the doctors said you had one week to live. It is now ten years; you are still alive.

The medical report said you could not have any children. You already had two pregnancies with twins; now, this is your third pregnancy, perhaps another twin, and they are all alive. You lost your job; instead of losing your mind, you got a better job.

The list is endless. Your responsibility is regulating your vain imagination, bad situation, or negative thoughts with your sanctified imagination. Apostle Paul calls it bringing into subjection, checking, or controlling every thought that exalts itself above the knowledge of God (2 Corinthians 10:5). Yes, you saw the destruction; you are aware of the doctor's report, but you sought the face of God. You are turning your vain imagination into a sanctified imagination.

In one of my books, I recount how the doctors said my mother wasn't going to live. In my vain imagination, I knew it was a fact. Nonetheless, in my sanctified imagination, I knew it was Satan's lie, and I refused to accept it. Moreover, I knew exactly what to do to change the situation "I PRAYED I USED MY ULTIMATE WEPON." and my mother lived to the astonishment of the doctors.

Yes, the report said you have cancer, but you know you are healed (1 Peter 2:24; Isaiah 53:5). You know you have no food, money, or dinner for your family, but you are confident God will provide (Genesis 22:8). The rent or mortgage is due and you have no money. Nevertheless, you are convinced God will supply your need (Philippians 4:19).

Forgiveness and Prayer

> And whenever you stand praying, if you have anything against anyone, forgive him that your Father in heaven may also forgive you your trespasses. But if you do not forgive, neither will your Father in heaven forgive your trespasses. (Mark 11: 25-26, NKJV)

Forgive us as we forgive those who offend us is an instruction. Your forgiveness is in proportion to how you forgive others (Luke 6:38). If you partly forgive, you will be partly forgiven. If you don't forgive, you can't access the forgiveness of God either (Matthew 6:14-15). Therefore, understand forgiveness is not an emotion. It is a decision!

You must forgive. You have a responsibility to totally forgive, no matter the pain. When you completely forgive somebody, it is not for them; it is for you. It is for your own good, wellbeing, and healthiness. When you forgive, you will feel as if a burden has been lifted off your mind. This was how I felt when I had an unusual experience in my office that got me livid. One of the managers deleted my vacation time and I was out of the country in Europe. When the direct deposit hit my account, it was half of what it should have been. I was hot!

Months after, I was still mad, irritated, upset and could not sleep. But God showed me Luke 6:28. I learned the importance of letting go and having peace in my heart so I could get some sleep.

Forgiveness facilitates answers to your prayers (Mark 11:25). It also allows you to walk in the fullness of God's love, mercy, forgiveness, and blessings. Did you know bitterness and unforgiveness will make you sick? Yes, they will literally make you sick. Our bodies and minds directly respond to unforgiveness. It is sin to be repented of.

Come and hear, all you who fear God, And I will declare what He has done for my soul.
I cried to Him with my mouth, And He was extolled with my tongue.
If I regard iniquity in my heart,

The Lord will not hear.
But certainly God has heard me;
He has attended to the voice of my prayer.
Blessed be God,
Who has not turned away my prayer, Nor His mercy
from me!
We come to the throne of grace
(Psalm 66:16-20, NKJV)

In the passage above, iniquity is equivalent to un-forgiveness. Iniquity is defined as immoral or grossly unfair behavior. In God's dictionary, this is sin. Some individuals are depressed and nursing suicidal thoughts because they can't forgive.

They won't let go whatever it is or whoever it is that hurt them. But if we confess our sins, God will forgive us.

"If we confess our sins, He is faithful and just to forgive us our sins and to cleanse us from all unrighteousness" (1 John 1:9).

Seeing then that we have a great High Priest who has passed through the heavens, Jesus the Son of God, let us hold fast our confession. For we do not have a High Priest who cannot sympathize with our weaknesses, but was in all points tempted as we are, yet without sin. Let us therefore come boldly to the throne of grace that we may obtain mercy and find grace to help in time of need.

(1 John 1:9- & 14-16, NKJV)

In conclusion, we have to make up our minds that no matter what the offense, we will forgive.

Ask

Give us this day our daily bread; Lead us not into temptation, but deliver us from the evil one "And in that day you will ask Me nothing. Most assuredly, I say to you, whatever you ask the Father in My name He will give you. Until now you have asked nothing in My name. **Ask**, and you will receive, that your joy may be full. (John 16:23-24, NKJV, emphasis mine)

God wants us to ask. He is waiting for us to ask as seen in verse 24 of the passage above. Having said that, in asking, you must also make sure whatever you are asking for lines up with God's will for you. Ask in line with the will and Word of God. If you don't know God's will, you have to find out what it is before asking in prayer for your desires.

This will prevent you from praying amiss as indicated in James 4:3. Remember to pray and ask in the name of Jesus Christ. This is essential because Jesus Christ is your link to God the Father. He is the only access to God as seen in John 14:6. When you ask in Jesus' name, God does not see you as you are but through the blood, death, and resurrection of Jesus Christ. We also ask in the name of Jesus Christ because His name has all power (Philippians 2:9-11).

The name of Jesus has healing, deliverance, and the answer to your needs. Let's see what the Scriptures say in John Chapter 14.

The Answered Prayer

Most assuredly, I say to you, he who believes in Me, the works that I do he will do also; and greater works than these he will do, because I go to My Father. And whatever you ask in My name, that I will do, that the Father may be glorified in the Son. 14 If you ask anything in My name, I will do it.

(John 14:12-14, NKJV)

We must ask in name of Jesus Christ because He went to the Father on our behalf (Hebrews 8:1; 1 John 2:1). When you pray and ask in line with God's will for you and according to His Word, the angels are waiting to execute the instructions from you. Hence, it is imperative you pray according to the will and Word of God. Praying with full knowledge and understanding of the will and Word of God facilitates speedy answers to your prayers.

When you are praying in the Word of God, the angels are attentive and will go forth to bring to pass what you are praying for (Daniel Chapter 3). But if you are not praying in line with the will and Word of God, the angels will not attend to you because no signals from you are on the heavenly radar indicating your desires. They only hear the Word of God and obey or take instructions according to the Word of God.

They do not respond to vain imaginations (Matthew 6:5-8). Thus, when we pray, we must get the scriptural foundation of what we are praying for as the base for asking and why our prayers must be answered.

> "He who did not spare His own Son, but delivered Him up for us all, how shall He not with Him also freely give us all things?" (Romans 8:32, NKJV).

God is committed to providing all of your needs and desires that line up with His Word and will for you.

"And my God shall supply all your need according to His riches in glory by Christ Jesus." (Philippians 4:19, NKJV). This Scripture points to the fact God isn't broke; He has unlimited resources to meet your needs.

God is omnipotent (all-powerful, almighty), omniscient (all-knowing), and omnipresent (ever-present, all-pervading). Whatever your questions and needs are, God has the answers in abundance through Jesus Christ. Simply put, Jesus Christ is the answer.

With this, we shall now examine the last key of the four key points in the "Lord's Prayer" as taught by Jesus Christ.

Yield

> "Thy kingdom come, Thy will be done (on earth as it is in heaven)"

Yield to the Holy Spirit. Romans 8:14 teaches all who are led by the Spirit of God are sons of God. In addition, Mark 14:36 demonstrated Jesus Christ yielded to the Holy Spirit in dying on the cross for the sins of the whole world.

> "And He said, 'Abba, Father, all things are possible for You. Take this cup away from Me; nevertheless, not what I will, but what You will'" (Mark 14:36, NKJV).

Four Ways to Yield to the Holy Spirit

The four ways to yield to or be led by the Spirit of God are,

1. Meditate on the Word of God. *"This book of the law shall not depart from your mouth, but you shall meditate in it day and night"* (Joshua 1:8, NKJV).

2. Be a doer of the Word of God. *"Be doers of the word and not hearers only"* (James 1:22, NKJV).

3. Put the Word of God above all else. *"My son, attend to my words; consent and submit to my sayings. Let them not depart from your sight; keep them in the center of your heart"* (Proverbs 4:20-21, AMPC).

4. Instantly respond to your spirit. *"The spirit of a man is the candle of the Lord"* (Proverbs 20:27, NKJV).

Summary

In the Lord's Prayer there are six requests grouped into two categories.

The first three requests are asking for the kingdom to come:

- Hallowed be thy name
- Thy kingdom come
- God's will be done

The second three are talking about God providing the needs of His people:

- Our daily bread
- Debts/trespasses
- Temptations

The highlight of the Lord's Prayer is deliverance. "But, deliver us from the evil one." Ask for deliverance from the Evil One (Satan) and all his traps.

Call to Action or Action Points

Always confess your faults one to another, and pray one for another, that ye may be healed. Furthermore, know that the effectual fervent prayer of a righteous man avails much (James 5:16).

Also understand,

- Prayer is the ultimate weapon.
- Prayer is a lifestyle, not an event.
- Prayer is an earthy license for heavenly interference.
- Prayer is believers giving God permission to interfere in earthly affairs.
- Prayer is believers giving heaven authority to perform God's Word on the earth.

Chapter 6

POWERFUL PRAYER PRINCIPLES

(Pray for All Men)

Therefore I exhort first of all that supplications, prayers, intercessions, and giving of thanks be made for all men, For kings and all who are in authority, that we may lead a quiet and peaceable life in all godliness and reverence. For this is good and acceptable in the sight of God our Savior, Who desires all men to be saved and to come to the knowledge of the truth. For there is one God and one Mediator between God and men, the Man Christ Jesus, Who gave Himself a ransom for all, to be testified in due time, for which I was appointed a preacher and an apostle I am speaking the truth in Christ and not lying a teacher of the Gentiles in faith and truth. I desire therefore that the men pray everywhere, lifting up holy hands, without wrath and doubting. (1 Timothy 2:1-8, NKJV)

"Powerful Prayer Principles" is the subject of my teaching in this chapter. But I want to give a visual illustration of the power of prayer before I start. Perhaps, everyone has a cell phone or a mobile phone. If not, you must have seen one. Now, if the cell phone is not connected to a power source to get charged, will it function? No!

The cell phone is useless and cannot work until it is connected to a power source, which charges the batteries. For your mobile phone to operate properly, you must occasionally connect it to the power source. Likewise, as Christians, we cannot function when we are not connected to our power source, Jesus Christ.

We must consistently plug into Him to function in this world. If we expect to fulfill our ministry (2 Timothy 4:5; Colossians 1:25) and accomplish our purpose on the earth, we must stay connected with

God always. We are useless and ineffective in this world without His help.

God created us with a unique purpose to be accomplished here on the earth. No two individuals, even twins, have the same purpose. Our purposes may converge at some point. Still, they aren't the same. If I am not connected to God to get instructions, how am I supposed to function effectively? To function effectively and efficiently in God's purpose for me, I must be connected to Him.

We connect to God through prayer. God created us to have a relationship with Him, to keep the relationship, we must pray. Hence, the Scriptures counsel us to pray without ceasing (1 Thessalonians 5:16-28). When your cell phones are not charged regularly, they run out of electrical energy and will not function. When you need them the most you realize they are dead.

Similarly, when, you are not connected to God the power source, you run out of spiritual energy to perform your purpose here on the earth. You know it is practically impossible to walk through the day without using your cell phone. So, you ensure it is always connected to the power source to be charged.

How do you expect to remain spiritually alive and energized without connecting or communicating with God? When you do not connect with God, you are empty and powerless. This was the case of Samson when he broke his connection with God (Judges 16:16-20).

How do you expect to accomplish those divine tasks without asking God for instructions? The only way to find out what God is saying is through prayer. Sometimes, you may be required to crosscheck some things with God to be sure you are in His perfect will. In line with this thought, I learned the following from 1 Timothy 2:1-8:

Praying for Everyone Is Not Praying about Everyone

Verse 1 – "Praying for all men"—the scriptures instruct us to demonstrate four of the seven principles we already studied. Here are the keys again for your convenience:

- Supplication (petition)
- Praise (reverence)
- Intercession (meditation)
- Thanksgiving (the attitude of gratitude – giving God praise)

Praying for everyone is not the same thing as praying about everyone. Praying for all people is praying for somebody because somebody prayed for you. Somebody had you on his/her mind and took the time to pray for you. You must pray for people, not about them. This allows you to see your weaknesses through the weaknesses of the people you are praying for. As you pray for others, God will show you, you! That means God will reveal your weaknesses to you. But praying about people creates the false sense of uprightness and self-holiness within you such that the person you are praying about becomes base. That is, you see yourself better than the person or people you are praying about (Luke 18:9-14).

When you find yourself in this situation, repent and confess your weaknesses to God. Likewise, when you pray for people and God reveals your weaknesses, repent and confess them.

Confession is good for the soul. It is good for building relationships whether with God or man. For some people, it is everybody's fault but theirs. Quit this "I am holier than you" attitude and accept you are wrong so you can be healed. When you are offended, learn from it and choose to forgive. Taking offense is a choice. You choose to be offended. You can also choose not to be offended. Nevertheless, if you are offended, choose to forgive because forgiveness is also a choice.

As you are praying for everybody, the Word of God and the Holy Spirit will show you who you really are. They are your inner probing lights that reveal your true personality.

For instance, when the flesh flairs up, you know it is the flesh because it will be accompanied by your emotions. Your flesh and emotions are like twins.

God has promised and will send you everything you need to accomplish your purpose here on the earth. Nothing can stop you from getting into the Promised Land and nobody can prevent you from entering the Promised Land. But you! Not the familiar gigantic Amalekites, Amorites, Hittites, Perizzites, Canaanites, Hivites, and Jebusites (Exodus 23:22-23) but those termites, foxes, and little sins inside of you (Song of Solomon 2:15; Hebrews 12:1; 1 Timothy 6:10-14).

Only you can stop you, so get out of your own way.

Verse 2 – we are instructed to pray for kings, those in authority—leaders both spiritual and secular. We are required to pray for the president, governors, and government officials. We must pray for our pastors, church leaders, and everybody in the leadership position. Pray for your managers, supervisors, coordinators, as well as the CEO or director of your company. Pray for them because the decisions they make affect our lives.

Secondly, as Christians, we know God is in control. They may think they are in charge. But the truth is, God is in control. Armed with the understanding God is in charge, we are confident when we pray, the atmosphere shifts and changes things. The scriptures corroborate this in Proverbs 21:1: *"The king's heart is like channels of water in the hand of the Lord; He turns it whichever way He wishes."*

In Ephesians 6:19 and Colossians 4:3-5, apostle Paul said, "Pray for me." He was in authority, so he needed the church to pray for him. Remember Peter was saved because the church prayed (Acts 12:5-17). Hence, we must pray for people in authority and pastors as well.

Verse 4 talks about praying for everybody to be saved. That is God's desire for the world. As kings and priests (1 Peter 2:9; Revelation 1:6; Revelation 5:10), we have the authority to pray for people to be saved. Where the word of a king is there is power

(Ecclesiastes 8:4). So, there is power and authority in your mouth. One of the ways we demonstrate this authority and power is by praying for others proclaiming God's will over them. God has given us dominion over the world (Genesis 1:26-28).

So, whatever you declare shall come to pass. As the Scripture says, you shall decree a thing; it shall be established (Job 22:28). Moreover, the Scriptures say *"Verily I say unto you, whatsoever ye shall bind on earth shall be bound in heaven: and whatsoever ye shall loose on earth shall be loosed in heaven"* (Matthew 18:18). And in praying for all men to be saved, the psalms say the following:

I will declare the decree: the Lord hath said unto me, Thou art my Son; this day have I begotten thee. Ask of me, and I shall give thee the heathen for thine inheritance, and the uttermost parts of the earth for thy possession. (Psalm 2:7-8)

God's desire for everybody is freedom from the oppression of Satan. Hence, He gave us the power to set the captives free, which Jesus Christ demonstrated when He delivered the folks who were sick, possessed of devils, oppressed by Satan in their minds, skin, and bodies. As a result, God gave us power as seen in the following scripture:

"Behold, I give unto you power to tread on serpents and scorpions, and over all the power of the enemy: and nothing shall by any means hurt you"
(Luke 10:19).

We are in warfare; it is the fight of faith (1 Timothy 6:12). We are not wrestling against flesh and blood, but against principalities, against powers, against the rulers of the darkness of this world, against spiritual wickedness in high places (Ephesians 6:12).

We also know, *"No weapon that is formed against us shall prosper, and every tongue that shall rise against us in judgment we shalt condemn. This is our heritage as the servants of the Lord, and our righteousness is of Him, says the Lord"* (Isaiah 54:17).

I have explained all six pieces of the armor we should have on daily. Get the CD or subscribe to my YouTube sermons and teachings to access them.

When you pray about a situation, you give God the permission to intervene in your affairs. Let us reexamine the concept of prayer and praying as stated in Ephesians 6:18-20.

Praying always with all prayer and supplication in the Spirit, being watchful to this end with all perseverance and supplication for all the saints And for me, that utterance may be given to me, that I may open my mouth boldly to make known the mystery of the gospel, For which I am an ambassador in chains; that in it I may speak boldly, as I ought to speak. (Ephesians 6:18-20, NKJV)

The Sheep and the Wolf

Praying for other people to be saved involves pastoring, mentoring, teaching, and correction. But among the sheep we pastor are wolves. We can pastor sheep but not wolves. Sheep and wolves in this usage represent the characters of some individuals. Most of the time, everyone pretends to be sheep displaying the humility that allows them to be pastored. However, there is the problem of not knowing the difference until the moment of correction. Whereas the sheep get in line, wolves' fangs come out. They start growling.

The first line of the anchor text for this series says, "Praying always with all prayer and supplication in the Spirit" (Ephesians 6:18). Praying in the Spirit is praying in power. We know God has made us a kingdom of kings and priests and has also given us dominion over the earth. Our responsibility is to rule in authority and power by prayer. Hence, we should understand,

1. Those who rule the earth know how to pray.
2. Our prayer must be empowered and directed by the Holy Spirit.
3. The Word of God and the Spirit of God must be in agreement. They work together. The Spirit of God is not going to lead you contrary to the Word of God. To pray effectively, we must know what the Word of God says.

The Ransom

Verse 6 talks about the ransom. Jesus Christ was the ransom. "Who gave himself a ransom for all, to be testified in due time" (1 Timothy 2:6). In other words, Jesus paid the price for you to have liberty here on the earth. Jesus Christ paid the price, so we have access to eternal life, fruitfulness, joy, peace, liberty, prosperity, security, good health, and everything God promised us in the Scriptures. This also gives us access to the power and authority we need when praying.

Holy Hands

In verse 8, the emphasis is on "holy hands." We pray everywhere lifting up holy hands without wrath and doubting. Holy hands mean consecration. Holy hands mean my hands are purified (Psalm 24:4). That is, I am washed by the blood of Jesus Christ. Lifting up holy hands is you saying, "Lord, my hands are clean and consecrated unto you; accept what I do with them."

Besides, when we lift up holy hands, we are saying, "God, inspect these hands; they are being used to glorify only You." By divine revelation, this can be interpreted as follows:

- I will not pursue things I should not seek after
- I keep my hands holy so I can lift them up in adoration to God.
- I can't worship God with bitterness, un-forgiveness, and doubt.

Without wrath means with "forgiveness" and without doubting means with "faith." It also means not being double-minded. We know a double-minded person is unstable in all of his ways (James 1:8). So, we must trust God. Our prayers are effective when we trust Him and pray in line with His Word. We have to know the Word, so we can pray the Word and get the results of the Word. But, if you don't know the Word, how are you going to pray the Word?

Let's look at somebody from the Scriptures who prayed the Word with amazing results. Our Bible example of a unique man who prayed the word with outstanding outcomes is Elijah. See what the Scriptures say about Elijah trusting God.

"Elijah was a man with a nature like ours, and he prayed earnestly that it would not rain; and it did not rain on the land for three years and six months" (James 5:17, NKJV cf.1 Kings Chapter 17).

Observe how the writer puts it, "Elijah was a man like us." This is what excites me about this scripture. Elijah was like you and me. He prayed and God honored his words. Likewise, when we pray, God will honor our words No matter how difficult. There is nothing too hard for God to do (Genesis 18:14; Jeremiah 32:17, 27) or impossible with God (Matthew 19:26; Luke 1:37).

Warning from God

During one of my Bible studies, I came across the following passage in the book of Deuteronomy, which was quite instructive and moving.

> Take heed to yourselves, lest your heart be deceived, and you turn aside and serve other gods and worship them, lest the Lord's anger be aroused against you, and He shut up the heavens so that there be no rain, and the land yield no produce, and you perish quickly from the good land which the Lord is giving you. (Deuteronomy 11:16-1 – 7, NKJV)

This was the warning of God when the people dwelled in sin, demonstrating Elijah knew the Word of God and his inspiration to shut the heavens for the sins of the people. As a result, he prayed the Word of God, and he got the results. In 1 Kings 18:41-46 based on 1 Kings 8:30-36, Elijah went back to God and prayed for rain and there was rain.

The Rain of God's Mercy

This passage teaches us when they turned from their sins, God released the rains (1 Kings 8:30-36). Now, what is your rain that has been shut?

The truth of God's Word is when we pray, the angels are alert so they can execute our instructions based on God's Word. The angels are commissioned and committed to executing your instructions as they minister to you (Hebrews 1:14). However, you first need to get it right with God. Thus, we need to develop the habit of praying regularly, seeking God's face for everyone.

The Role of the Holy Spirit in Prayers

Likewise the Spirit also helps in our weaknesses. For we do not know what we should pray for as we ought, but the Spirit Himself makes intercession for us with groanings which cannot be uttered. Now He who searches the hearts knows what the mind of the Spirit is, because He makes intercession for the saints according to the will of God. And we know that all things work together for good to those who love God, to those who are the called according to His purpose. For whom He foreknew, He also predestined to be conformed to the image of His Son, that He might be the firstborn among many brethren. Moreover whom He predestined, these He also called; whom He called, these He also justified; and whom He justified, these He also glorified.

(Romans 8:26-30, NKJV)

God has already called you, and the Holy Spirit is interceding for you. He is praying for you. You know you don't always have it together, so, you need His help. As we continue with this teaching, say this simple prayer:

"Lord, help me! Lord, help me.
Lord, help me with me!"

Praying in the Holy Spirit requires us to be baptized in the Holy Spirit with the evidence of speaking in tongues. We need the Holy Spirit to fight for us in spiritual warfare, pulling down strongholds, casting down imaginations, every high thing that exalts itself against the knowledge of God and bringing into captivity every thought to the obedience of Christ (2 Corinthians 10:4-5).

Know that in your spirit, the weapons of our warfare are mighty through God to pull down strongholds. Thus, we must pray in the Spirit and be consecrated—set apart.

Praying in the Spirit

Praying in the Spirit (Ephesians 6:18) simply means not praying in the flesh (1 Corinthians 12:8-11). Although many people don't want to agree, praying in the Spirit is praying in your heavenly language, deep calling unto deep. They are both inspired by the Holy Spirit.

Thus, praying in the Spirit introduces the element of the supernatural or the spiritual (not ecstasy but godliness) and honesty into praying. As the Scriptures say, "God is a Spirit: and they that worship him must worship Him in Spirit and in truth." This suggests praying or prayers engage the mind, soul, and spirit.

Three Kinds of Tongues

1. Heavenly language prayer (1 Corinthians 14:2) praying to God
2. Praying in languages you did not learn— diverse tongues like French (Acts 2:4-8)
3. Prophetic tongues, word from the Lord that should have an interpretation (1 Corinthians 14:14-15 & 26)

Praying in the Spirit also means praying according to the will of God. Praying according to the will of God lets the Holy Spirit pray through you. As you pray in the heavenly language, you are praying a perfect prayer.

Consecration, Self-Consciousness, God-Consciousness

Praying in the Spirit comes after consecration. When you are consecrated, you become less self-conscious and more God-conscious. On the other hand, self-consciousness means you want to do the things you like to do. God-consciousness means you are responding to the leading of the Holy Spirit (Romans 8:14-17) doing what God wants you to do as an obedient child.

Praying in the Holy Spirit and in tongues is predicated on your consecration. Consecration means to be set apart for God's purpose. It results in less self-consciousness and more of God-consciousness.

Recall Romans 8:26 teaches praying in the Spirit builds you up. The Holy Spirit helps you to develop the things that are not yet developed in you, particularly your personality. The Holy Spirit will reveal to you the things you know you have, the things you don't know you have, and the things you don't want other people to know you have.

Hence, the Scriptures say The Holy Spirit convinces the world concerning sin, righteousness, and judgment (John 16:8), teaches you all things, and brings all things to your remembrance (John

14:26). The Holy Spirit will confront you with all your weaknesses. That is to say, the Holy Spirit will show you, you.

The Holy Spirit makes intercession for you inside of you. Before you are consecrated cleansing, which is washing is done. You are cleansed through Word of God (John 15:3; Ephesians 5:26) and through the blood of Jesus Christ (Matthew 26:28; Hebrews 9:22; 1 John 1:7; Revelation 1:5).

As you continue to let the Holy Spirit pray for you, you are continuously consecrated. The Holy Spirit is always willing to pray for you, but you must allow Him to do so. Remember He makes intercession for us with groanings that cannot be uttered. In the gospel according to Matthew, Jesus Christ said:

> O Jerusalem, Jerusalem, the one who kills the prophets and stones those who are sent to her! How often I wanted to gather your children together, as a hen gathers her chicks under her wings, but you were not willing! (Matthew 23:37, (NKJV)

God wants to bless you but you refuse to get in line. He wants to gather you like a hen gathers her chicks but you would not let Him.

Birds of the Same Feathers Flock Together

"Birds of the same feathers flock together" is an old English adage that was also quoted by Benjamin Franklin. It signifies like attracts like. Individuals with similar behaviors tend to relate and flock with each other the same way birds of the same species flock together.

While this phrase can be understood in moral terms, the biblical parallel highlights that broken people naturally gravitate to individuals who are broken where they are broken. The closest Bible references are Psalm 119:63; Matthew 7:16-18, and 2 Corinthians 6:14.

You can tell who you are by who you like. Gossipers will gravitate to other gossipers. Messy people will hook up with other messy people. Drama queens will like other drama queens. Liars will be attracted to other liars. That is to say what you befriend you agree with.

Having received the baptism of the Holy Spirit, it behooves you to allow Him to search your heart. He knows what is going on with you and why. The good news is the Holy Spirit will bridge the gap between you and the Promised Land.

Corporate Prayer

The final concept to be discussed in this chapter is corporate prayer and its relevance, particularly in the church. In Acts Chapter 12, Peter was kept in a maximum-security prison under the instruction of King Herod. We discussed this in Chapter 5 and here we have it again.

Peter was therefore kept in prison, BUT constant prayer was offered to God for him by the church. And when Herod was about to bring him out, that night Peter was sleeping, bound with two chains between two soldiers, and the guards before the door were keeping the prison. Now behold, an angel of the Lord stood by him, and a light shone in the prison; and he struck Peter on the side and raised him up, saying, "Arise quickly!" And his chains fell off his hands. Then the angel said to him, "Gird yourself and tie on your sandals"; and so he did. And he said to him, "Put on your garment and follow me." So he went out and followed him, and did not know that what was done by the angel was real, but thought he was seeing a vision. When they were past the first and the second guard posts, they came to the Iron Gate that leads to the city, which opened to them of its own accord; and they went out and went down one street, and immediately the angel departed from him. And when Peter had come to himself, he said, "Now I know for certain that the Lord has sent His angel, and has delivered me from the hand of Herod and from all the expectation of the Jewish people." So, when he had considered this, he came to the house of Mary, the mother of John whose surname was Mark, where many were gathered together praying. (Acts 12:5-12)

Pray for All Men

The conjunction "but" as seen in verse 1 above changed everything. Observe Peter thought he was in a dream. He was released from prison by an angel who was attending to the corporate prayer of the disciples. As the Scriptures teach, one can send a thousand to flight …two will put ten thousand to flight (Joshua 23:10; Deuteronomy 32:30 compare Leviticus 26:8). The prayers of the church changed the situation.

Peter was awaiting execution in prison. James had already been killed and it pleased the Jews. So, Peter was taken. If the church refuses to pray corporately for the church leaders: apostles, prophets, evangelists, pastors, and teachers

(Ephesians 4:11), the Enemy will devour the leaders one after the other.

Accordingly, apostle Paul advocates the relevance of praying for all men as he personally asked the church to pray for him (Acts 4:24-29; Ephesians 6:18-19, Colossians 4:3; 2 Thessalonians 3:1-5).

Can you recite this scripture one more time?

Therefore I exhort first of all that supplications, prayers, intercessions, and giving of thanks be made for all men, for kings and all who are in authority, that we may lead a quiet and peaceable life in all godliness and reverence. For this is good and acceptable in the sight of God our Savior, who desires all men to be saved and to come to the knowledge of the truth. For there is one God and one Mediator between God and men, the Man Christ Jesus, who gave Himself a ransom for all, to be testified in due time, for which I was appointed a preacher and an apostle—I am speaking the truth in Christ and not lying—a teacher of the Gentiles in faith and truth. I desire therefore that the men pray everywhere, lifting up holy hands, without wrath and doubting;

(1 Timothy 2:1-8, NKJV) ~ Pray for All Men

Chapter 7

Prayer, Fasting, and Giving

Many people say God knows what they need. He just needs to intervene. No, beloved. According to the Scriptures, you must ask; invite Him into your circumstance.

"Ask, and it will be given to you; seek, and you will find; knock, and it will be opened to you. For everyone who asks receives, and he who seeks finds, and to him who knocks it will be opened"
(Matthew 7:7-11).

My sisters and brothers, the three concepts ask, seek, and knock must be complete for God to intervene in your situation.

When You Pray

And when you pray, you shall not be like the hypocrites. For they love to pray standing in the synagogues and on the corners of the streets, that they may be seen by men. Assuredly, I say to you, they have their reward. But you, when you pray, go into your room, and when you have shut your door, pray to your Father who is in the secret place; and your Father who sees in secret will reward you openly. And when you pray, do not use vain repetitions as the heathen do. For they think that they will be heard for their many words. Therefore do not be like them. For your Father knows the things you have need of before you ask Him. (Matthew 6:5-8)

Observe the Scriptures above didn't say "if you pray" but "when you pray." Now, let's proceed to when you fast.

When You Fast
Fasting to Be Seen Only by God

Moreover, **when you fast**, do not be like the hypocrites, with a sad countenance. For they disfigure their faces that they may appear to men to be fasting. Assuredly, I say to you, they have their reward. But you, **when you fast**, anoint your head and wash your face, so that you do not appear to men to be fasting, but to your Father who is in the secret place; and your Father who sees in secret will reward you openly. (Matthew 6:16-18, emphasis mine)

Giving
Lay Up Treasures in Heaven

Do not lay up for yourselves treasures on earth, where moth and rust destroy and where thieves break in and steal; but lay up for yourselves treasures in heaven, where neither moth nor rust destroys and where thieves do not break in and steal. For where your treasure is, there your heart will be also. (Matthew 6:19-21)

You Cannot Serve God and Riches

"No one can serve two masters; for either he will hate the one and love the other, or else he will be loyal to the one and despise the other. You cannot serve God and mammon" (Matthew 6:24).

Points to note in the scripture

The Model Prayer

Those who pray with improper motives (Matthew 6:5-7)

Fasting to Be Seen Only by God

Matthew 6:16 –18

You Cannot Serve God and Riches

Money can't be your God (Matthew 6:24)

Praying Is a Choice

Matthew Chapter 6 presents three principle elements of the effectual fervent prayer of the righteous: praying, fasting, and giving. As said earlier, it didn't say if you pray but when you pray. When you pray is premised on the fact you are going to pray as instructed in Ephesians 6:18 and 1 Thessalonians 5:16-18. It is under the impression you are going to pray in obedience.

Then it says you cannot serve two masters. You cannot serve God and mammon. Mammon in the Scriptures means money. When you serve money, you are a slave to it because you yield to it. So, you cannot serve God.

We said in the last chapter under the definition of P-R-A-Y the Y represents Yield. That is, you are required to yield to God. Whatever you yield to owns you. Whether it is sin, money, or God. You have a choice to make. However, we discover in this teaching instead of sin or money, you yield to God so you can serve Him. When you serve God, you cannot serve money.

At some point in your Christian journey, you may have to choose between God and money. There will be a conflict of interest. Accepting the money may hinder you from serving God and you will have to choose between the two. You cannot straddle the fence; it is one or the other.

When you pray for God to intervene in your circumstances, you are praying for heavenly interference in your earthly affairs. If your situation has not changed then you need to fast. As you fast, you must give, sowing some precious seed.

"Those who sow in tears shall reap in joy. He who continually goes forth weeping, bearing precious seed for sowing, shall doubtless come again with rejoicing, bringing his sheaves with him"

(Psalm 126:5-6).

We must sow seeds toward our expectations. So, when we pray, fast, and give, we can expect the manifestation of whatever it is we are seeking God's intervention for. Thus, you can be assured of the manifestation of everything God promised you, not something or a few things—everything God has promised you.

When we pray, we are inviting God into our situations, but sometimes that doesn't work. So you have to fast. Then, you have to give. Don't give up saying God doesn't answer prayers. When you need a breakthrough in your life, pray, fast, and give. If you need the manifestations of God's Word in your life, pray, fast, give. Likewise, if you need freedom from strongholds that have you bound pray, fast, and give.

Giving

I will not go through the entire concept of giving in this book. For more in-depth reading on this subject that will help you understand God's mind about giving, read "GIVING~ God's Divine exchange rate."

The Scriptures clearly teach the importance of giving and its benefits. We should give tithes, the first fruit, the offering, and alms. So, as presented in the Bible, when you give, particularly tithe, you must expect to receive. The Scriptures confirm this as follows:

> "Give, and it will be given to you: good measure, pressed down, shaken together, and running over will be put into your bosom. For with the same measure that you use, it will be measured back to you" (Luke 6:38, NKJV).

When it comes to tithing, you either give it or steal it. It is your choice. Your tithe, the 10 percent of your income and the firstfruit of your increase belong to God. This implies when you give God your 10 percent. He is committed to blessing your remaining 90 percent.

God said when you tithe, He will open the windows of heaven and pour blessings upon you so you will not have enough space for storing them. But notice He went further to say prove me now. In other words, He is saying try Me now. Not later, not when you finish paying your mortgage, not when you change your job, not when your children are grown and you have no school fees to pay. God said prove me now if I will not confirm my word in your life. Recognize, this is the only verse of Scripture in which God asks us to challenge (have the courage or guts) Him as the Sovereign God. Let's get into the Scriptures to confirm this in the book of Malachi.

> Bring all the tithes (the whole tenth of your income) into the storehouse, that there may be food in My house, and prove Me now by it, says the Lord of hosts, if I will not open the windows of heaven for you and pour you out a blessing, that there shall not be room enough to receive it. (Malachi 3:10, AMPC)

> Bring the full amount of your tithes to the Temple, so that there will be plenty of food there. Put me to the test and you will see that I will open the windows of

> heaven and pour out on you in abundance all kinds
> of good things. (Malachi 3:10, GNT)

Then, we have the firstfruit (Deuteronomy Chapter 26). The Scriptures teach us to give or honor the Lord with our substance and with the firstfruit of all our increase (Proverbs 3:9). The firstfruit of your increase is when you get, for instance, a 30% (percent) increase in your wages. The first thirty percent of the increase (which is the difference between your old salary and new salary) in the first month of the increase is the first fruit of your increase. When you give your firstfruit to God, you are saying Lord, I trust you with my resources.

As said earlier, when we tithe, we expect multiplication because the result of giving your firstfruit is increase or multiplication as seen in this scripture.

> "Honor the Lord with your possessions, And with the
> firstfruits of all your increase; So your barns will be
> filled with plenty, and your vats will overflow with
> new wine" (Proverbs 3:9-10, NKJV)

Having said that, you can only have firstfruit in the harvest season. Firstfruit has both literal and symbolic significance and relevance. Jesus Christ was recorded as the firstfruit from the dead.

> But now Christ is risen from the dead, and has become the firstfruits of those who have fallen asleep. For since by man came death, by Man also came the resurrection of the dead. For as in Adam all die, even so in Christ all shall be made alive. But each one in his own order: Christ the firstfruits, afterward those who are Christ's at His coming.
>
> (1 Corinthians 15:20-23)

You have to define the firstfruit of your increase.

Then, we have the offering and the seed. Talking about the seed and the sowing of seeds, Scripture says when you sow your seed, you should expect a hundredfold, some sixty, some thirty multiplication in your harvest (Mark 4:20).

> "But these are the ones sown on good ground, those who hear the word, accept it, and bear fruit: some thirtyfold, some sixty, and some a hundred"
>
> (Mark 4:20).

This is to say when you sow your seed, sometimes you get 30 percent of your harvest; other times you get 60 percent, and finally, 100 percent of your harvest. The beauty is something always comes up. But if you have no seed in the ground, nothing will grow.

If no seed is in the ground, how can you expect a harvest? Our economy is no longer a predominantly agriculture-based economy where our livelihoods are purely from farming (crop farming and animal farming). Our economy is now mixed. Now, we earn most of our income as salaries or wages. So 30%, 60%, and 100% increase in the harvest could come as an increase in wages, promotion in your job or a new and better job.

Finally, let's look at the giving of alms, which means giving to the poor. The giving of alms also attracts God's blessings. So, when you give alms, you should have the expectation God will give back to you as much as you gave, knowing the measure you give is the measure you get.

"Give, and it will be given to you: good measure, pressed down, shaken together, and running over will be put into your bosom. For with the same measure that you use, it will be measured back to you" (Luke 6:38).

Summary of Giving

1. Tithes – you are giving it or stealing it!
2. First fruit – showing God your gratitude for the blessings He has bestowed upon you. Thanksgiving for God's provision
3. Offering/seed – sowing to reap the harvest in 30, 60, and 100-fold
4. Almsgiving – not given to God but to man

Prayers

I have done several teachings on prayers. In the last teaching, we said the word pray is an acronym: Praise, Repent, Ask, and Yield. I talked about the different kinds of prayers, the prayer of supplication, and prayer of thanksgiving and prayer of the petition are some examples. I talked about putting on the whole armor of God in (Ephesians 6:10-20).

Then, I talked about being watchful to the end. I said being watchful to the end means an attitude of resilience and tenacity. Your mindset is "I am going to watch until I see the manifestation of what I am praying for." The last point I talked about was the powerful principles of prayer.

We have talked about giving and prayer. I am now going to discuss fasting. Before we look at some scriptures about fasting, let's get its proper definition.

Fasting

Fasting is the willful abstaining from natural pleasures for a spiritual purpose. Pleasure can be sex, food, sport, television, and entertainment. That means when fasting, I am not on a diet. The difference between fasting and dieting is the purpose. Dieting is done to lose weight, keep physically fit, and healthy. Fasting is done for spiritual reasons, to pull down strongholds, free you from bondage, and change situations. Yes, in the process, you will lose weight, but it is not dieting.

Thus, when you fast, you abstain from natural pleasures. Fasting is done for a spiritual purpose. As a result, the Scriptures teach,

"For bodily exercise profits a little, but godliness is profitable for all things, having promise of the life that now is and of that which is to come. This is a

faithful saying and worthy of all acceptance"
(1 Timothy 4:8-9).

Two of Our Strongest Desires Are for Food and Sex

Two of the strong desires we have as human beings are the desire to eat and to have sex. So, abstaining from these two desires gets us into a position where we can hear from God and become beneficiaries of His move. Fasting does not move God but it prepares you for the move of God.

Most of the time, single ladies and men have a problem with the desire to have sex. God created sex to be done in the confines of marriage, not outside marriage. So, you don't need fast to stay away from fornication, you need self-control (Galatians 5:22-23; 1 Corinthians 9:27; 2 Peter 1:6).

Recognize a War Is Going On

Satan, the Enemy, is progressively aggressive and seeking to destroy you (John 10:10; 1 Peter 5:8-9). If he can't get a hold on you he goes for your job, your loved ones, anything he can use to derail your relationship with God. Thus, apostle Paul in his letter to the Ephesians teaches we wrestle not against flesh and blood but against principalities, powers, the rulers of the darkness of this world, and spiritual wickedness in high places. In spiritual warfare, the weapons of our combat are not scientific but spiritual (2 Corinthians 10:4-5).

Three Levels of Heaven

There are three levels of spiritual warfare in heaven.

1. The third heaven is where God dwells.
2. The second heaven is where you have the angels.
3. The first heaven is the atmosphere.

God has given us dominion and authority to change the atmosphere (Genesis 1:26-28; Luke 10:19; Luke 24:49; Acts 1:8; Matthew 28:18-20). You decide what happens on the earth.

> Verily I say unto you, Whatsoever ye shall bind on earth shall be bound in heaven: and whatsoever ye shall loose on earth shall be loosed in heaven. Again I say unto you, that if two of you shall agree on earth as touching anything that they shall ask, it shall be done for them of my Father which is in heaven. (Matthew 18:18-20, KJV)

Be Dressed and Be Prepared

As I said in an earlier chapter, you can't fight spiritual battles with natural means. In a spiritual battle, we are required to fight spiritually. There are two invisible kingdoms. The kingdom of God and the kingdom of Satan and that these two kingdoms are constantly in warfare. You must choose which one you belong to.

If you are a Christian, you are in the kingdom of God. Being on the Lord's side or in the Lord's army naturally makes you an enemy of Satan and pitches you in warfare against the kingdom of Satan. If you want to conquer, you must wear the whole armor of God (Ephesians 6:10-20).

The Principle of Answered Prayer

Some of the problems you encounter can only be broken by fasting and prayer. Knowing you are in continuous warfare, you must put on the full armor of God and always be prepared so you can win. Now, let us get into the Scriptures starting with the book of Matthew.

And when they were come to the multitude, there came to him a certain man, kneeling down to him, and saying, Lord, have mercy on my son: for he is lunatick, and sore vexed: for ofttimes he falleth into the fire, and oft into the water. And I brought him to thy disciples, and they could not cure him. Then Jesus answered and said, O faithless and perverse generation, how long shall I be with you? how long shall I suffer you? bring him hither to me. And Jesus rebuked the devil; and he departed out of him: and the child was cured from that very hour. Then came the disciples to Jesus apart, and said, Why could not we cast him out? And Jesus said unto them, Because of your unbelief: for verily I say unto you, If ye have faith as a grain of mustard seed, ye shall say unto this mountain, Remove hence to yonder place; and it shall remove; and nothing shall be impossible unto you. Howbeit this kind goeth not out but by prayer and fasting. (Matthew 17, 14- 21)

The disciples couldn't get the man's son delivered as seen in the passage above because of unbelief and the lack of fasting. Jesus Christ said we will do greater works than He did. Meaning, we will not stop where Jesus Christ stopped. Rather, we will do what He did and even more.

Most assuredly, I say to you, he who believes in Me, the works that I do he will do also; and greater works than these he will do, because I go to My Father. And whatever you ask in My name, that I will do, that the Father may be glorified in the Son. If you ask anything in My name, I will do it. (John 14:12-14)

Unbelief prevents us from doing greater works. We don't believe what the Word of God says. God guarantees when we act in faith, He will bring our instructions to pass. No matter how difficult your situation may seem, nothing is too difficult for God to do (Genesis 18:14). He said, "I am not a man that, I should lie."

"God is not a man, that He should lie, Nor a son of man, that He should repent. Has He said, and will He not do? Or has He spoken, and will He not make it good?" (Numbers 23:19).

"Is anything too hard for the Lord? At the appointed time I will return to you, according to the time of life, and Sarah shall have a son" (Genesis 18:14).

For as the rain comes down, and the snow from heaven, and do not return there, but water the earth and make it bring forth and bud, that it may give seed to the sower and bread to the eater. So shall My word be that goes forth from My mouth; it shall not return to Me void, but it shall accomplish what I please, And it shall prosper in the thing for which I sent it. (Isaiah 55:10-11)

"Behold, I am the Lord, the God of all flesh. Is there anything too hard for Me?" (Jeremiah 32:27)

"But Jesus beheld them, and said unto them, with men this is impossible; but with God all things are possible" (Matthew 19:26)

"For with God nothing shall be impossible"
(Luke 1:37).

"Again I say to you that if two of you agree on earth concerning anything that they ask, it will be done for them by My Father in heaven" (Matthew 18:19).

The preceding Scripture verses establish God is committed to His Word. I deliberately listed them to arouse your faith that if you act, God will confirm His Word (Mark 16:17-20; Hebrews 2:3-4). So, if God said it, it is done.

Fasting Is to be Done for a God-centered, Biblical Purpose.

Fasting is not a human idea. It is God's idea. God inspires fasting through the Holy Spirit. God said we should fast. Fasting is to be done for a God-centered biblical purpose. Your fast should not be self-centered. When your purpose or motives are right you should be able to fast with amazing results.

You should be successful in what it is you are fasting or fasted for. I said fast with amazing results because some folk fast without any results. A God-centered fast demands we have a need or the object or subject of the fast and Scripture to back them up. Holding onto scriptures during a fast helps to overcome hunger. Instead of focusing on your hunger and rumbling stomach you meditate or reflect on the scriptures concerning the need you are fasting for.

Fasting Is God's Ideal (Not Self-Centered)

Fasting is God's ideal; it is not self-centered. Fasting is for you! That means you don't fast to delight or influence God. You cannot manipulate God. In fact, manipulation is like witchcraft. We can't manipulate through fasting. We fast to put our flesh under subjection (1 Corinthians 9:27).

We put our flesh under subjection to get our minds focused on God. We don't fast to amaze God either. This is because fasting does not impress God.

Fasting is to be done for God-centered biblical purposes and not to impress Him. We are expected to have a lifestyle of fasting. When you fast, your body and mind go through a harsh experience. Your stomach will growl; you will suddenly develop a migraine, and definitely, you will be weak.

Despite, these experiences, know that fasting strengthens your prayers. Moreover, the beauty about fasting for God-centered purposes is as you persist and are determined, you suddenly discover the rumbling in your stomach has ceased; the migraine is gone, and you feel great inside. Here is how to manage the fasting process:

- When your stomach growls, it is a reminder to pray.
- When you get a headache, it is a reminder to pray.
- When it is lunchtime, it is a reminder to pray

Different Kinds of Fast

Normal Fast – no food, water only, normally done for about three days. In the scriptures, you are not told how long to fast because that is between you and God.

Absolute Fast – absolutely no food or water. Again I caution this should not be undertaken over 3 days, except you have a clear directive from the Lord and are in good health.

Daniel Fast (Daniel 1:12-15) – sometimes called partial fasting, this is when you abstain from certain meals of the day or eating certain kinds of foods during your fast (no meat or sweets, soup only, fruit and vegetables only, etc.).

In Daniel 10:3, Daniel ate no pleasant food. No meat or wine entered his mouth. He did not anoint himself at all for three weeks. "Did not anoint himself" means he did not apply any cream to his body. For ladies this could mean no makeup. For instance, you eat one meal a day with a certain type of food.

These are the major fasts in the Bible. If God called you to do a forty-day fast, it is for a special purpose. The majority of Christians don't fast for forty days. Jesus Christ fasted for forty days. Abraham also fasted for forty days.

Scientists have come up with a theory that the human body can sustain a forty-day fast, after which, your body takes a hit and you proceed to starvation.

Corporate Fast

This is when the church or a group of people feel God has called them to fast together for a certain period. Let's examine the following two scriptures on the corporate fast.

Jeremiah Calls for a Corporate Fast

Now it came to pass in the fifth year of Jehoiakim the son of Josiah, king of Judah, in the ninth month, that they proclaimed a fast before the Lord to all the people in Jerusalem, and to all the people who came from the cities of Judah to Jerusalem. Then Baruch read from the book the words of Jeremiah in

> the house of the Lord, in the chamber of Gemariah
> the son of Shaphan the scribe, in the upper court at
> the entry of the New Gate of the Lord's house, in the
> hearing of all the people. (Jeremiah 36:9-10, NKJV)

In the passage above, Jeremiah the prophet called everybody to a fast. As they all gathered, they expected God to move on their behalf because of the fast that was called.

Another corporate fast with Bible evidence is in the book of Esther.

Esther Calls for a Corporate Fast

> Then Esther spoke to Hathach, and gave him a com-
> mand for Mordecai: "All the king's servants and the
> people of the king's provinces know that any man
> or woman who goes into the inner court to the king,
> who has not been called, he has but one law: put
> all to death, except the one to whom the king holds
> out the golden scepter, that he may live. Yet I myself
> have not been called to go in to the king these thirty
> days." So they told Mordecai Esther's words. think in
> your heart that you will escape in the king's palace
> any more than all the other Jews. For if you remain
> completely silent at this time, relief and deliverance

will arise for the Jews from another place, but you and your father's house will perish. Yet who knows whether you have come to the kingdom for such a time as this?" Then Esther told them to reply to Mordecai: "Go, gather all the Jews who are present in Shushan, and fast for me; neither eat nor drink for three days, night or day. My maids and I will fast likewise. And so I will go to the king, which is against the law; and if I perish, I perish!"

(Esther 4:10- 16 – NKJV)

Esther, a Jewish lady, the wife of King Ahasuerus (Esther 2:15-18), was called to the palace at a unique time (4:14) to deliver the Jews in Shushan. Harman got an edict from the king to destroy all the Jews in Shushan (Esther 3:8-15). Mordecai, Esther's uncle, informed Esther of the plan.

Esther recognized the deliverance of her family and her people was in her hand and if she didn't act, they would all perish. Consequently, she called for a corporate fast as she was going to break the rules to see the king uninvited (Esther 4:15-17), which usually attracted the death penalty.

The corporate fast is when we come together as a church, family, or group in a fast, seeking God's intervention for a specific need. As we fast corporately, we have the expectation God will intervene. It is very important when a corporate fast is called everyone participates. As said before, Scripture teaches one can put a thousand to flight, and two will put ten thousand to a flight (Deuteronomy 32:30).

Corporate prayers and fasts allow the body of Jesus Christ, the church, to accomplish more. It helps us to achieve greater works as the Scriptures say (John 14:12-14). Besides, Scripture teaches when two people agree (Matthew 18:19-20) what they ask for shall be given. Hence, it is essential to have a corporate fast as a church, family, business, or nation.

Benefits of Fasting

We have established that fasting is done according to God's purpose, and it is intended to bring our bodies under subjection. Accordingly, fasting can help us break certain habits and develop new ones. Fasting also helps us to overcome sin and live acceptable to God.

If you discover you are a victim of a particular sin or bad habit despite your honest effort to curb it through prayers and self-control, you should fast. I delineate more on the benefits of fasting at the conclusion of this book.

Common Sin and Besetting Sin

I said fasting helps us to break certain habits and sins. For this purpose, we shall group sins into two classes as common sins and besetting sins. This grouping is not intended to grade sins in higher or lower levels. It is done to expose and explain the nature of sin and how to manage it. Understand there are no hierarchies to sin. All sin carries the same weight and punishment from God.

Common sins could be sins of pride, idolatry, murder, dishonesty, and jealousy to mention but a few. Note in the Scriptures, the sin of murder is not only when you take somebody's life. It includes when you use your mouth to rundown somebody (backbiting and gossip). Thus, you commit murder with your mouth.

Learn to Keep Your Mouth off God's People

A scriptural example of common sin was the sin of the people of God that led to their exile in the foreign land of Babylon.

Common Sin (Scriptural Evidence)

> In the first year of his reign I, Daniel, understood by the books the number of the years specified by the word of the Lord through Jeremiah the prophet that He would accomplish seventy years in the desolations of Jerusalem. Then I set my face toward the Lord God to make request by prayer and supplications, with fasting, sackcloth, and ashes. And I prayed to the Lord my God, and made confession, and said, "O Lord, great and awesome God, who keeps His covenant and mercy with those who love Him, and with those who keep His commandments, we have sinned and committed iniquity, we have done wickedly and rebelled, even by departing from Your precepts and Your judgments. (Daniel 9:2-5, NKJV)

The common sins of the people of Israel were revealed in verse 5. These sins resulted in their exile for seventy (70) years.

Besetting Sin

This could be a persistent bad habit. A constant problem or recurrent fault, smoking and alcoholism, are two of such habits we often find difficult to quit. The way to break such a habit is prayer and fasting. *"Howbeit this kind goeth not out but by prayer and fasting"* (Matthew 17: 21).

I was addicted to smoking weed. I wanted to stop, I knew I had to stop, but I just couldn't. I kept telling myself I will stop smoking weed. However, the more I said I will stop smoking, the more I realized I couldn't stop.

Then I discovered my mind was ready to stop but, I didn't have the willpower to stop. It was as if it were beyond my power to stop smoking weed. My dilemma was similar to apostle Paul's impasse as seen in the following scriptures.

> For what I am doing, I do not understand. For what I will to do, that I do not practice; but what I hate, that I do. If, then, I do what I will not to do, I agree with the law that it is good. But now, it is no longer I who do it, but sin that dwells in me. For I know that in me (that is, in my flesh) nothing good dwells; for to will is present with me, but how to perform what is good I do not find. For the good that I will to do, I do not do; but the evil I will not to do, that I practice. Now if I do what I will not to do, it is no longer I who do it, but sin that dwells in me. (Romans 7:15-20)

I was held in this unpleasant experience for a long time until I discovered from the Word as seen in Romans 7: 20 what the problem was. I knew what I had to do to destroy the bondage of smoking weed. I engaged accordingly and I had my freedom.

Fasting will break the grip of any besetting sin in your life. Common sin is easy to repent from compared to besetting sin. Still, on the sin dilemma, there are two desires: the desires of the flesh and godly desires.

The desires of the flesh are what you want outside the purpose and will of God. Godly desires are God's desires for you.

Having said that, it is important to know all sin is the same in God's eyes. A thief is no "better" than a murderer, so we are no "better" than anyone else. God, through the Scriptures, expresses His desire for us to repent from all sin, even the besetting sins.

Wherefore seeing we also are compassed about with so great a cloud of witnesses, let us lay aside every weight, and the sin which doth so easily beset us, and let us run with patience the race that is set before us, looking unto Jesus the author and finisher of our faith; who for the joy that was set before him endured the cross, despising the shame, and is set down at the right hand of the throne of God. (Hebrews 12:1-2)

Spiritual Crisis and the Call to Repentance

When you are in a spiritual crisis, you need to repent and seek the face of God.

Now, therefore," says the Lord, "Turn to Me with all your heart, With fasting, with weeping, and with mourning."

So rend your heart, and not your garments; Return to the Lord your God, For He is gracious and merciful, Slow to anger, and of great kindness; And He relents from doing harm.

Who knows if He will turn and relent, And leave a blessing behind Him— A grain offering and a drink offering For the Lord your God?

Blow the [a]trumpet in Zion, Consecrate a fast, Call a sacred assembly;

Gather the people, Sanctify the congregation, Assemble the elders, Gather the children and nursing babes; Let the bridegroom go out from his chamber, And the bride from her dressing room.

Let the priests, who minister to the Lord, Weep between the porch and the altar; Let them say, "Spare Your people, O Lord, And do not give Your heritage to reproach, That the nations should [b]rule over them. Why should they say among the peoples, 'Where is their God?' " (Joel 2:12 – 17)

There was a spiritual crisis, a situation in Israel that needed to be solved through corporate prayer and fasting. Accordingly, Joel called a fast that involved everybody. This fast did not exempt anyone, even nursing mothers were involved.

But in the case of Daniel, as seen Daniel 9:2-5, he stood in the gap, prayed and fasted for the repentance of his people, so they could be free from the oppression of the Babylonians.

Examining the scriptures above, you discover God gives us an opportunity to repent. Repentance could be defined as an outward feeling of penitence for wrongs which is accompanied by a change of heart and sorrow for sin.

There are three steps to repentance:

1. Acknowledge your sin
2. Turn away from your sin (what are you doing?)

3. Turn toward God doing whatever He wants you to do.

Fasting That Pleases God

Yet they seek Me daily, And delight to know My ways, As a nation that did righteousness, And did not forsake the ordinance of their God. They ask of Me the ordinances of justice; They take delight in approaching God.

'Why have we fasted,' they say, 'and You have not seen? Why have we afflicted our souls, and You take no notice?' "In fact, in the day of your fast you find pleasure, and exploit all your laborers.

Indeed you fast for strife and debate, and to strike with the fist of wickedness. You will not fast as you do this day, to make your voice heard on high.

Is it a fast that I have chosen, A day for a man to afflict his soul? Is it to bow down his head like a bulrush, and to spread out sackcloth and ashes? Would you call this a fast, And an acceptable day to the Lord?

"Is this not the fast that I have chosen: To loose the bonds of wickedness, To undo the [c]heavy burdens,

To let the oppressed go free, And that you break every yoke?

Is it not to share your bread with the hungry, And that you bring to your house the poor who are [d] cast out; When you see the naked, that you cover him, And not hide yourself from your own flesh?

Then your light shall break forth like the morning, Your healing shall spring forth speedily, And your righteousness shall go before you; The glory of the Lord shall be your rear guard.

Then you shall call, and the Lord will answer; You shall cry, and He will say, 'Here I am.' "If you take away the yoke from your midst, The [e]pointing of the finger, and speaking wickedness,

If you extend your soul to the hungry And satisfy the afflicted soul, Then your light shall dawn in the darkness, And your [f]darkness shall be as the noonday.

The Lord will guide you continually, And satisfy your soul in drought, And strengthen your bones; You shall be like a watered garden, And like a spring of water, whose waters do not fail. (Isaiah 58:2-11, NKJV)

The Benefits of Fasting Continued

In closing this book, here is a list of what fasting will do for you, but **only** when your motives align with the will of God for your life. These scriptures will help you pray the right prayers when you fast for a need.

- Break the yoke of poverty and the supernatural (Job 23 and Joel 3:13)
- Solve problems (Isaiah 58:6 and Ezra Chapter 8)
- Intimacy with God (Matthew Chapter 9)
- Ark of the Covenant (1 Samuel 7:6)
- Revelation/Clear perspective (Acts 9:9-18)
- Supernatural power (Luke 4:1-2) Holy Spirit 40-day fast
- Discernment for a spouse (Genesis Chapter 24)
- Break the spirit of grief
- Hannah (1 Samuel)
- David (2 Samuel Chapter12)
- Knowing the will of God (Acts Chapter 13)
- Ordain leaders/ministry gifts (Acts Chapter 14)
- Protection from the Enemy (Esther Chapter 4)

The Duration of Fast

Finally, note, the scriptures didn't tell us how long or how often we should fast. Even if the Bible doesn't tell you, if you ask God, He will. To find out how long and how often you should fast, you should ask God.

Why not ask Him today? Realize some things will not change or manifest in your life unless you pray, fast, and give. But if you pray, fast, and give you will see the manifestation of the Word of God.

For God is faithful.

Key Points to Takeaway

- Prayer, fasting, and giving attract divine manifestation.
- If you need a breakthrough in your life pray, fast, and give.
- To see the manifestation of God's Word in your life, pray, fast, give.

Chapter 8

CONCLUSION

Overview of Prayer

This chapter culminates the teaching series on *The Ultimate Weapon Is Prayer Inviting Heaven to Intervene in Earthly Affairs.*

What Is Prayer?

I started this teaching with the unique question "What is prayer?" Your answer to this exclusive question about prayer will determine the success of your Christian journey with God here on the earth. Now it's time to move ahead with learning the secrets of answered prayer.

I hope after reading this teaching series on the ultimate weapon is prayer, you will be able to take control of your destiny, directing the affairs of your life, family, marriage, ministry, church, business, education, job, and career by engaging the "ultimate weapon of prayer." I pray this becomes a fruitful walk in the end.

Run-walk

Recall I said was going to "walk" you through this prayer journey. I intentionally chose the word "walk" as I do not intend to create the false impression you can rush through this Christian race.

Success in any learning is a process that involves several dynamics. The Christian race is one of those where you need to learn with patience, confidence, resilience, and tenacity. The Christian journey by nature is warfare; only those who are resilient and tenacious achieve success.

Therefore, you must learn everything that makes it a good success (Joshua 1:8). Then again, those with microwave oven orientation, who are always on the fast lane, often discover the race is not that simple.

I will encourage you to take time to learn every concept there is about prayer. It is essential to learn every step there is when becoming a prayer warrior. Learn as much as you can, and prudently travel this road because it lasts for a lifetime.

It is not a short-distance race like the 100-meter race you take in school—not at all! Neither is it a leisure walk in the park. No, it has to be a dedicated, purposeful, and consistent walk for there to be worthwhile results. Run-walk this journey because you will require strength, valor, fortitude, and above all, faith, as the anchor for success.

Looking unto Jesus Christ

On this journey, your focus is Jesus Christ, the Author and Finisher of your faith (Hebrews 12:2). He is the one that will supply all the above qualities needed to run-walk this journey. You need Jesus Christ to become a warrior in prayer.

> Let us keep our eyes fixed on Jesus, on whom our faith depends from beginning to end. He did not give up because of the cross! On the contrary, because of the joy that was waiting for him, he thought nothing of the disgrace of dying on the cross, and he is now seated at the right side of God's throne.
>
> (Hebrews 12:2, GNT)

> Looking away [from all that will distract] to Jesus,
> Who is the Leader and the Source of our faith [giving
> the first incentive for our belief] and is also its Fin-
> isher [bringing it to maturity and perfection]. He, for
> the joy [of obtaining the prize] that was set before
> Him, endured the cross, despising and ignoring the
> shame, and is now seated at the right hand of the
> throne of God. (Hebrews 12:2, AMPC)

I have used these two different translations to stress the relevance of incorporating and becoming resolute in Jesus Christ for the success of your life of prayer. When you focus on Jesus Christ, you will enjoy the fellowship and help of the Holy Spirit. Then, you will understand what prayer is, and what it takes to live a life full of it.

Praying Is the Will of God

The Christian's need for prayer has never been so relevant than in our contemporary society. In view of the recent happenings, one cannot but agree with Cristy Lane when she sang "One Day at a Time." In the song, Cristy acknowledges the times are much more difficult now than when Jesus Christ was here on the earth.

One day at a time, sweet Jesus
I'm only human, I'm just a woman
Help me believe in what I could be and all that I
am
Show me the stairway I have to climb
Lord, for my sake teach me to take one day at a
time

One day at a time, sweet Jesus
That's all I'm asking from You
Just give me the strength to do everyday
What I have to do
Yesterday's gone, sweet Jesus
And tomorrow may never be mine
Lord, help me today, show me the way
One day at a time

Do you remember when You walked among men?
Well Jesus, You know, if You're looking below, it's
worse now than then
Cheating an stealing, violence and crime
So for my sake, teach me to take one day at a
time

One day at a time, sweet Jesus
That's all I'm asking from You

Just give me the strength to do everyday
What I have to do
Yesterday's gone, sweet Jesus
And tomorrow may never be mine
Lord, help me today, show me the way
One day at a time
(Lane, Cristy, "One Day at a Time")

Scripture warned in the last days men will be lovers of pleasure and will recruit preachers who will tell them what they like to hear. The wicked will increase (2 Timothy Chapter 3). Still, as pointed out in the introduction of this book, it is our responsibility to take dominion over the earth and bring down heavenly influence into the affairs of men.

> "Thy kingdom come, thy will be done on earth as it is in heaven" (Matthew 6:10).

Defining "Pray" and "Prayer"

From this teaching series, I said prayer is an acronym delineated as follows.

P-R-A-Y-E-R. Positive Reassuring Action Yielding Eternal Results

P – Positive: this means being optimistic and confident.

R – Reassuring: prayer reassures us of God's commitment to His promise.

A – Action. Prayer is an activity that involves doing what God expects you to do to unlock His promised blessings (Mark 11:23-24).

Y – Yielding. In prayer, you set your will aside and submit to the will of God.

E – Eternal. The prayer we said is heavenly interference in earthly affairs. Thus, the results of praying are eternal. Knowing the gifts and calling of God are without repentance (Romans 11:29).

R – Results. As already mentioned, when you pray, be expectant because God is committed to providing answers to your prayer requests (John 14:13-14). I also said the word pray is an acronym as seen here. P-R-A-Y - Praise, Repentance, Asking for others, as well as asking for yourself.

As I said before, when asking, your focus should not be you only but on those around you as well. This will demonstrate the love of God. Learn to stand in the gap for someone in prayer. We saw in Ezekiel 22:30-31 God wanted someone to intercede for the people but there was no one. To confirm we get more done when we pray for one another. Deuteronomy 32:30 highlights one person praying can chase a thousand, but two people will put ten thousand to flight.

Develop the habit of praying for others and always ask others to pray for you. Esther was a good example of a wonderful lady who asked for prayers (Esther 4:15-16).

Apostle Paul is another interesting preacher who always asked the church to pray for him (Romans 15:30-33; 2 Corinthians 1:10-11; Ephesians 6:19-20; Philippians 1:19-20; Colossians 4:2-4; 1 Thessalonians 5:25; 2 Thessalonians 3:1-2; Philemon 22).

Do not depend on people to intercede for you. Instead, get into the habit of praying for yourself.

Praise, Repent, Ask, and Yield

To pray means to Praise, Repent, Ask, and Yield. I developed this acronym from the model of prayer

Jesus Christ gave to His disciples when they asked Him to teach them how to pray. As mentioned, the secret to a successful ministry and the victorious life in Jesus Christ is prayer (Matthew 6:9-13; Luke 11:1-13).

Interestingly, the Bible doesn't give any account of when Jesus Christ prayed with His disciples. Therefore, instead of asking for power or wisdom like Solomon (1 Kings 3:1-15), they asked for prayer. Asking to be taught how to pray surpassed asking for wisdom because when you know how to pray, you will have wisdom.

Here, is a quick recap of the prayer Jesus Christ taught His disciples and was intended to teach us as well. Taking this model from Matthew 6:9-13, there are four basic elements in the prayer, summarized as follows: praise, repentance from sins, asking God, and yielding to God's will.

It is therefore apparent every prayer we pray must have these four elements to meet the standard of prayers required of us. As a reminder, here is the breakdown once more.

Praise: Hallowed be the name of our Father in heaven; for thine is the kingdom, and the power and the glory, forever.

Repent: Forgive us our sins, as we forgive those who sin against us.

Ask: Give us this day our daily bread; Lead us not into temptation, but deliver us from the evil one.

Yield: Thy kingdom come, thy will be done (on earth as it is in heaven)

This order is very essential to arranging our prayers as it will prevent us from praying with the wrong motives (James 4:3).

Two Invisible Kingdoms

When I started these teachings on prayer, I said there were two invisible spiritual kingdoms. The kingdom of God and the kingdom of Satan, I said these two kingdoms were continuously at war with each other.

I then contrasted these two invisible kingdoms. Demonstrating the roles they play in the lives of Christians and said the mind was the battlefield.

God Is Calling Us to a Lifestyle of Prayer

Understand the call to salvation is a call to the lifestyle of praying as your salvation is not sustainable without consistent prayers and fellowship with God the Father, the Son, and the Holy Spirit. As pointed out earlier, the theme of the book *The Ultimate Weapon is Prayer* came about from apostle Paul's letter to the church in Ephesus through divine revelation. Here is the scripture again.

"Praying always with all prayer and supplication in the Spirit, being watchful to this end with all perseverance and supplication for all the saints" (Ephesians 6:18).

"For we do not wrestle against flesh and blood, but against principalities, against powers, against the rulers of the darkness of this age, against spiritual hosts of wickedness in the heavenly places" (Ephesians 6:12).

Apostle Paul, in this letter, talked about spiritual warfare. He explained this spiritual warfare is not a battle to be won with the conventional weapon of war (2 Corinthians 10:4-6; Ephesians 6:12-17). Furthermore, he stated this battle is a wrestle, not with flesh and blood (fellow human beings and what we can see and feel) but with the unseen world of darkness of spiritual forces operating and controlling the first heaven.

Remember we said there are three levels of heavens. God dwells in the third heaven (2 Corinthians 12:2).

Recall when Daniel prayed in Daniel 9:1-19, the angel who delivered the answers to his prayers narrated to him how the prince of the kingdom of Persia prevented him for 21 days until Michael the Archangel came to his defense (Daniel 10:10-14). He made it clear to Daniel he would fight his way back to God. He even added the prince of Greece will follow the prince of Persia. But he said the Archangel Michael would defend him.

> Then he said, "Do you know why I have come to you? And now I must return to fight with the prince of Persia; and when I have gone forth, indeed the prince of Greece will come. But I will tell you what is noted in the Scripture of Truth. (No one upholds me against these, except Michael your prince
>
> (Daniel 10:20-21).

Four Components of Demonic Activities

The four components of demonic activities operate from the kingdom of Satan. Take the time to learn and understand these four components of demonic activities because these are the forces we war against.

> "For we do not wrestle against flesh and blood, but against [1] **principalities**, against [2] **powers**, against the [3] **rulers of the darkness of this age**, against [4] **spiritual hosts of wickedness in the heavenly places**" (Ephesians 6:12, emphasis mine).

Principalities

Principalities are ranked demons. They forcefully take possession of a region and create a domain exercising authority over the region. This region could be a nation, marriage, and business.

The demonic influence they create could be war, despair, greed, and lack of contentment.

Powers

Powers are spiritual authorities with the capacity to control and spellbind. Examples of Satan's power are fortune-telling, clairvoyance, sorcery, the occult, and magic. Remember the witch of Endor (1 Samuel 28:7-20)

The third and fourth entities are the rulers of the darkness of this age and spiritual hosts of wickedness in the heavenly places. Whereas rulers of the darkness of this age are deceptive spirits, the spiritual hosts of wickedness in the heavenly places are territorial powers (Daniel 10:12-12). These powers control the heavenly places.

These are the four components of demonic activities every Christian wars against. To discern when the kingdom of darkness is warring against you, you must be deeply rooted in prayer.

Prayers create the right atmosphere for you to communicate with the Holy Spirit dwelling inside of you, who will reveal the kingdom of Satan and his pranks.

The Battlefield of the Mind

The scriptures teach above all else, guard your heart, for everything you do flows from it (Proverbs 4:23). If Satan gets your heart, he already has your mind. When he deceived Eve (2 Corinthians 11:3) and tempted Jesus Christ (Matthew 4:1-11; Luke 4:1-13), it all started in the mind.

Satan is described as a thief, murderer, and deceiver (John 10:10; John 8:44; Revelation 12:9), which means he takes advantage of your weaknesses and strikes when you are defenseless. He disarms innocent individuals by taking hold of their minds.

His goal is to capture your heart because he knows once he gets hold of your heart, you are now under his control. Thus, you become his tool. Much like you see in a game of chess; the complete purpose of the game is to capture the king.

So, whatever moves you see on the chessboard have one aim: to get hold of the king. Likewise, Satan's pranks are exclusively designed to arrest your heart. When he succeeds, you become his instrument of destruction (Genesis 4:1-8). Perhaps you have heard the saying the idle mind/brain is the Devil's workshop as much as the idle hands are his tools. That means the unengaged mind or the empty mind is the Devil's workshop as seen in the following scriptures.

When an unclean spirit goes out of a man, he goes through dry places, seeking rest, and finds none. Then he says, 'I will return to my house from which I came.' And when he comes, he finds it empty, swept, and put in order. Then he goes and takes with him seven other spirits more wicked than himself, and they enter and dwell there; and the last state of that man is worse than the first. So shall it also be with this wicked generation. (Matthew 12:43-45)

The scripture above is a lucid illustration of somebody who was delivered from the oppression of Satan; the unclean spirit goes out. The next step was to fill the vacuum with the Word of God and the Holy Spirit. But this was not done.

As a result, the demon came back with his team. Satan will always attack your mind. Every sin starts from the mind. Therefore, to win spiritual warfare, you start from the mind and win in the mind.

The Relevance of Prayers

Prayer is important to your spiritual life as the air is important to your physical life. Our need for prayer to function in our divine estates is as important as our need for air to breathe. God, in His creation, set the hierarchies and arranged the pattern of dominion and authority for the earth.

God did not make man first because of this divine hierarchy. He created man as the climax of

His work to take charge and act like Him. Thus, the man was God's ambassador on the earth.

He was serving as God's warden to the people and the people's warden to God. Communication was carried out through the medium of prayer as demonstrated by Jesus Christ.

Apostle Paul, also having been mandated by God to occupy the apostolic office, understood the need of prayer. Thus, by revelation, he wrote we should pray without ceasing as this is the will of God (1 Thessalonians 5:16-18).

After the creation, God handed over the world to man through Adam. Adam was given full authority in the earth realm, and God will not override Adam's authority. This means when God said, "Let man rule...over all the earth" (Genesis 1:26), He was commanding, controlling, and arranging the powers and authorities on the earth to make the role of the church fundamental for the accomplishment of His purposes.

He rearranges earthly events in favour of the church, the body of Jesus Christ when men and women pray in agreement with His will and Word. Therefore, prayer is indispensable for accomplishing God's will on the earth. The prophet Isaiah confirmed this when he prophesied.

> Many people shall come and say, "Come, and let us go up to the mountain of the Lord, To the house of the God of Jacob; He will teach us His ways, And we shall walk in His paths." For out of Zion shall go forth the law, And the word of the Lord from Jerusalem. (Isaiah 2:3, NKJV)

Thus, the church was mandated to control and direct the affairs on the earth. The instrument to demonstrate this headship over the affairs on the earth is praying. God's majestic design was for the church to depend on Him for their sustenance.

Since the garden of Eden, man rebelled against the leadership of God. This was pronounced when the people of Israel demanded a king (1 Samuel Chapter 8). Right from the garden, God never intended man should provide for himself.

Hence, He provided the angels to minister to us (Hebrew 1:14; 2:1-4) and the Holy Spirit to help us accomplish our tasks here on the earth (John 14:14-26). Christianity is not DIY (Do It Yourself). Subscribe to God to use and enjoy His blessings. Serving God is a decision, so is praying.

Types of Prayers

Prayer, as we have identified, is the ultimate weapon. However, for it to work effectively, you must be trained in its use. You cannot properly operate a weapon you are not trained to use.

When David was to face the giant warrior, the Goliath of Gath (1 Samuel Chapter 17), King Saul dressed him in the customary military gear. But David couldn't use them, not necessarily because they were very heavy but he was not trained in their use (1 Samuel 17:38-39).

Nonetheless, he took his sling because he was trained to use it; he had gained mastery and acquired years of experience in its use. Thus, David destroyed the giant warrior, the Goliath of Gath, not with a sword but with a sling.

> So Saul clothed David with his armor, and he put a bronze helmet on his head; he also clothed him with a coat of mail. David fastened his sword to his armor and tried to walk, for he had not tested them. And David said to Saul, "I cannot walk with these, for I have not tested them." So David took them off.
>
> (1 Samuel 17:38-39, NKJV)

So it was, when the Philistine arose and came and drew near to meet David, that David hurried and ran toward the army to meet the Philistine. Then David put his hand in his bag and took out a stone; and he slung it and struck the Philistine in his forehead, so that the stone sank into his forehead, and he fell on his face to the earth. So David prevailed over the Philistine with a sling and a stone, and struck the Philistine and killed him. But there was no sword in the hand of David. (1 Samuel 17:48-50, NKJV)

"The ultimate purpose of this book is to help you understand prayer inside out."

Now, we know the different types of prayers, their meanings, and how to engage them in spiritual warfare to win our battles against Satan. As we conclude this book, understand there are no clear differences between these different kinds of prayers.

The majority of these different types of prayers can be blended to match the prevailing circumstances for success and efficacy.

One of the scriptures we examined in these teachings with these fundamentals is in the apostle Paul's letter to Timothy.

> Therefore I exhort first of all that supplications, prayers, intercessions, and giving of thanks be made for all men, for kings and all who are in authority, that we may lead a quiet and peaceable life in all godliness and reverence. For this is good and acceptable in the sight of God our Savior, who desires all men to be saved and to come to the knowledge of the truth. For there is one God and one Mediator between God and men, the Man Christ Jesus, who gave Himself a ransom for all, to be testified in due time, for which I was appointed a preacher and an apostle—I am speaking the truth in Christ and not lying—a teacher of the Gentiles in faith and truth.
>
> (1 Timothy 2:1-7, NKJV)

As highlighted earlier, the need to pray is more expedient now in the history of mankind than before. Thus, praying for everyone in response to the scriptures above is mandatory.

> "Praying always with **all prayer and supplication** in the Spirit, being watchful to this end with all perseverance and supplication for all the saints."
>
> (Ephesians 6:18 - NKJV)

As we round up, let's decide to always pray in the Holy Spirit with all prayers and supplications. Since my desire is to get you to the point where you meditate on prayer before praying, I also want to quickly recap how prayer should look even before you pray.

1. Prayer is a lifestyle, not an event.
2. The effective, fervent prayer of a righteous man avails much.
   a. Effective mean successful in producing the desired result
   b. Fervent means having or displaying a passionate intensity

Prayer Doesn't Have to be Loud or Long

Prayer doesn't have to be loud or long. However, it can be both when the Holy Spirit is leading you. Likewise, passion doesn't mean you always pray in a loud voice or the prayer has to be very long.

Introduction to the next book *Promises of God*

Have you prayed for a need based on God's promises, but instead of a solution, your predicament became worst? Did you know based on the promises of God you cannot be broke? There are numerous promises of God in the Scriptures.

But how do you know these promises are yours? How do you appropriate these promises in your life? How do you activate these promises of God?

On this point let me quickly mention prayer is one of the ways you activate the promises of God. Hence, the next teaching after the prayer series is on the promises of God.

ABOUT THE
AUTHOR

Senior Pastor Teresa S. McCurry

P *astor Tee was called* to ministry in 2010 under the leadership of Apostle Leon and Pastor Margie Nelson. She has traveled extensively, educating and inspiring others with her unique approach to holistic solutions for ministry leadership, self-care, and kingdom development.

This was the beginning of a great and powerful deliverance move of God in her life to reach the hurting and lost. God anointed Pastor Tee with spiritual eyesight and the ability to speak into people's lives. Immediately, deliverance takes place to bring forth healing to broken-hearted souls, to proclaim liberty to the captives, and set their hearts completely free.

Pastor Tee is dedicated to helping people who seek to make positive changes.

Her marketplace ministry extends beyond the walls of the church. She is a Beauty Entrepreneur, Inspirational Speaker, International Bible Teacher and International Bestselling Author. She is a licensed cosmetologist with over 30 years of beauty industry experience. She holds a Bachelor's degree in Applied Business Administration. Teresa's passion for the beauty industry standards is displayed in the excellence with which she leads by example educating, serving, and beautifying clients while inspiring them to reach their God-given purpose.

Teresa's discipleship is personal and unscripted. She is prophetic in nature and led by the Holy

Spirit. What she offers is leadership training that is personalized to each of her disciple's unique situations and needs. She works with a limited number of clients each year in a few different ways: Personal Discipleship, Signature Group Discipleship Coaching, and PTU ~ Pastor Tee University (Coming Soon).

Her literary work has resulted in her being recognized as a highly acclaimed best-selling author who has traveled internationally speaking to leaders around the globe in countries such as China, South Africa, Europe, and the Caribbean. She is noted for equipping leaders with relevant tools to enhance leadership mechanisms to lead in love.

Her marketplace ministry extends beyond the walls of traditional church settings, which includes being an industry leader as a Beauty Entrepreneur, Inspirational Speaker, and International Bible teacher.

Pastor Tee is an emerging philanthropist, who is passionate about reaching underserved communities. This passion birthed the MCS Fund, which is a 501 © 3 nonprofit organization dedicated to providing financial support and advocacy for individuals affected by sickle cell disease. In 2020, she received an honorary doctorate for Humanitarianism from Global International Alliance, by authority of the

International Association of Christian Counselors.

Pastor Tee holds a Bachelor of Arts in Applied Business Administration from Bryant & Stratton College. She resides in Northeast Ohio, with her loving husband, Apostle Greg McCurry, where they co-labor as a ministry team at New Beginning Ministries.

Appendix

www.blueletterbible.org
www.gotquestions.org
https://www.biblegateway.com
bible.org
enduringword.com/bible-commentary
www.workingpreacher.org
biblehub.com
www.thepassiontranslation.com